An A
for Your Palate

Coastal Connecticut
Waterfront Dining
with Chefs' Recipes

By Judith Errichetti Sulik

Finely Finished Press

Bridgeport, Connecticut

2000

Copyright ©2000 Judith E. Sulik
Cover Art Copyright © 2000 Joseph M. Sulik

All Rights Reserved.
No part of this book may be reproduced or copied in *any* format without
permission of the publisher except for the inclusion of brief quotations
in a review.

ISBN 0-9657193-3-2

Finely Finished Press
60 Acton Road, Bridgeport, CT 06606
yduj@juno.com

First Printing 2000

10 9 8 7 6 5 4 3 2 1

*Note: Although the recipes, restaurant descriptions, directions to
the restaurants, and historical notes have been carefully edited and
checked for accuracy, the publisher cannot be held responsible for
any errors in same; or by spoiled ingredients, unsanitary condi-
tions, incorrect preparation procedures or any other cause beyond
their control. All recipes have been printed exactly as given to the
author by the restaurants. The recipes have not been retested and
the author and publisher are not responsible for errors of any type.*

Acknowledgments

Thank you to the restaurant owners, chefs, and staff for their cooperation in making this book a reality and especially to David Poirior of the Connecticut Historical Commission for providing the historical marker descriptions that introduce each town along the Constitution State's shore; and to Sharon Dina and Francine Fielding, for proofreading and recipe checking. And to everyone — friends, family and strangers — who listened to me during the evolution of this project, I am forever grateful.

This book is dedicated to my parents,
Rocco and Helen Errichetti,
whose enthusiasm for the open road
and adventure inspiring.

Author's Note

For a copy of Connecticut Boater's Guide, which lists boat launch locations, write to DEP Boating Division, P.O. Box 280, 333 Ferry Rd., Old Lyme, CT 06371-0280 or call 860-434-8638. Visit http://dep.state.ct.us/rec/parks.htm for information about Connecticut state parks and forests.

Contents

Contents (continued)

5

Introduction

Connecticut has 618 miles of tidal shoreline, but while the 111.6 mile long Interstate 95 roughly follows the shoreline connecting Stonington, near Rhode Island, with New York's neighbor, Greenwich, finding Long Island Sound from the highway is not easy. Unless one knows which exit to take, finding one of the many restaurants offering waterfront dining is truly an adventure.

Restaurant owners and chefs provided the recipes in this book; most were not tested *and they were published as given*. As Madame Benoit said, "... a recipe is only a theme, which an intelligent cook can play each time with a variation." A narrative derived from interviews with the owner accompanies each restaurant's recipes. The *Guide to Services* tells at a glance if a child's menu is offered, boat docking available nearby, etc. Unfortunately, the restaurant business is very fluid, so information is only accurate as we go to press; confirmation that the restaurant is still in operation is recommended. It is possible I missed some restaurants; my intention was to encourage travelers to leave the highway for a culinary adventure along Connecticut's shore — everything seems to taste better when enjoyed with a waterfront view.

If you doubt traveling today "could be worse", consider this verse written by Sarah Knight who spent five months traveling on horseback from Boston to New York in 1704, surviving bad roads, miserable taverns, and the rudeness of the times:

> *Now I've returned to Sarah Knight's*
> *Thro' many toils and many frights,*
> *Over great rocks and many stones,*
> *God has prearv'd from fractured bones.*

Whether by land or by sea, Connecticut's shoreline towns still offer travelers an adventure, but one unlike anything Sarah could have imagined. I hope you enjoy using this book as much as I enjoyed researching and writing it.

Judith Sulik

Greenwich

Adriaen Block, a Dutch explorer, sighted these shores in 1614. This was then the land of the Petuquapaen or Siwanoy Indian tribe, a branch of the Mohegans. On July 18, 1640, Daniel Patrick and Robert Feake purchased from the Siwanoys, in the name of the New Haven Colony with 25 English coats, the land between Asamuck and Patomuck brooks, now the area of Old Greenwich. From 1640 to 1642 Greenwich was an established settlement under English rule. From 1642 to 1656 it was Dutch under the manor system. In the latter year Greenwich again became English, governed by Stamford in the jurisdiction of the New Haven Colony, and nine years later was granted town status by the consolidated colonies of Connecticut and New Haven. In 1672, 27 heads of families purchased all lands between the Myanos and the Byram rivers from the few remaining Indians. This area became known as the Horseneck Plantation, now central Greenwich.

ATLANTIS
500 Steamboat Rd., Greenwich
(203) 861-1111

Atlantis is the first (or last) waterfront restaurant along Connecticut's western coast.

Breakfast, lunch, and dinner are served seven days a week, a convenience much appreciated by the guests at the adjoining 97 room hotel, the Greenwich Harbor Inn.

While American seafood specialities predominate on the menu, other choices are also offered. Live musical entertainment at night reaches beyond the standard rock 'n roll repertoire to include calypso, reggae, and jazz. While listening to the music, the 600-foot long dock gives boat watchers a lot of interesting watercraft to drink in.

In addition to the restaurant, tiki bar, deck, and inn, *Atlantis* also has a banquet room that can provide service for private parties of 250 people.

At *Atlantis*, the management says, "We're proud of our restaurant. We serve excellent food in a tastefully decorated atmosphere."

And all in a room with a view.

TARTAR OF TUNA
ON CORN BASIL SALAD

TUNA TARTAR

12 oz. fresh tuna filet
1 small red onion,
chopped
1 bunch chives, chopped
8 T. soy sauce

3 T. sesame oil
1 T. Dijon mustard
Salt
Fresh ground pepper

Mix tuna medium-fine in a food blender. Add the rest of the ingredients, seasoning to taste, and mix well.

CORN BASIL SALAD

2 fresh ears of corn
Milk and salt for cooking
corn
6 basil leaves, julienned

8 T. olive oil
2 T. champagne vinegar
Fresh ground pepper
Salt

4 basil leaves for garnish

Cook the corn in milk and salt for about 15 minutes. Remove the kernels from the cob while still warm; cool down in the refrigerator. When the corn is cold, mix all of the ingredients together.

Make 4 patties of the tuna and place the corn in the middle of the plate. Put the tuna on the top and garnish with a basil leaf.

Serves four

SESAME CRUSTED
SWEET WATER PRAWNS

4 sweet water prawns or large shrimp, peeled and deveined
¼ C. soybean oil
1 T. sesame seeds
1 clove garlic, sliced
1 t. sliced fresh ginger root
10 oz. shiitake mushrooms

2 T. finely sliced vegetables (carrots, celery, sweet pepper, leeks)
2 T. rice wine vinegar
2 T. soy sauce
2 T. honey
1 blood orange, segmented
1 piece of celery leaf

Baste the prawns with some of the soybean oil and roll them in the sesame seeds. Sear the prawns in a hot pan until the sesame seeds are golden. Remove them from the pan and finish cooking in a pre-heated oven at 375° for about 5 minutes.

Add the remainder of the oil to the pan and add the garlic, ginger, shiitake mushrooms, and sliced vegetables. Sauté quickly and add the vinegar, soy sauce, and honey.

Remove the vegetables from the pan and place in the middle of a plate. Arrange the prawns around the vegetables and spoon extra sauce over the top.

Garnish with the blood orange segments and the celery leaf.

Serves one

CHOCOLATE PECAN KISSES

2 sheets of phyllo pastry cut into 4"x 2" rectangles	2 oz. dark chocolate
	2 T. brown sugar
¼ C. melted butter	¼ C. pecan halves
2 oz. white chocolate	¼ C. golden raisins

Pre-heat the oven to 375°.

Finely chop the white and dark chocolates.

Brush three pieces of the phyllo pastry with the melted butter.

Place the pieces on top of each other in a star formation. Repeat process using remaining phyllo.

Combine the rest of the ingredients in a small bowl.

Place a ¼ of the chocolate mixture into the middle of the pastry sheets.

Pull the sides of the pastry together and pinch to form a purse.

Bake in the pre-heated oven for 3 to 4 minutes.

Makes four kisses

Stamford

Purchased from Ponus, sagamore (chief) of Toquama, and Wascussue, sagamore of Shippan, July 1, 1640, by Nathaniel Turner, agent of New Haven Colony.

In May 1641, town was settled by a company of 28 families from Wethersfield under leadership of the Reverend Richard Denton. First called Rippowam, was renamed Stamford in 1642 from Stamford in Lincolnshire, England, included all of present Darien; Pound Ridge, New York; part of New Canaan.

Stamford men participated in the American Revolution, and Fort Stamford, now a city park, was erected in 1781 to defend the area. Stamford was primarily agricultural until the arrival of the railroad in 1848.

CRAB SHELL
46 Southfield Ave., Stamford Landing, Stamford
(203) 967-7229

Crab Shell's owners, Dick Gildersleeve and Jim Clifford, pay attention to the little things. For example, recognizing that many people would like to dine al fresco well into the cooler season, they have installed heat lamps so diners can stay warm. And martini glasses are kept on ice on the bar top. And they urge people to call and find out if this is the week they are having a clambake or buffet dinner or to learn what band is performing.

People who are curious about what goes on in a restaurant kitchen can get a first hand look at *Crab Shell*: the display kitchen brooks no secrets. Dick said their goal is "to be a casual basic seafood restaurant; no fancy sauces; just good value and good portions." The *Crab Shell* goes to great lengths to bring regional specialities to Stamford. Depending on the time of year, you may find stone crabs, Maryland blue crabs, Dungeness crabs from the Northwest, Boston cod — the list goes on.

The *Crab Shell* takes full advantage of its waterside location — half of the walls are glass and every table overlooks either the water or the marina. Dick says simply that "the decor is the outdoors."

FLORIDA STONE CRAB CLAWS
WITH MUSTARD SAUCE

2 lb. fresh Florida stone crab claws, about 8-10 large claws	1½ t. Worcestershire sauce
5 oz. mayonnaise	3 T. sour cream
1½ T. Dijon mustard	¼ t. dry mustard
	½ t. chopped parsley

Crack the crab claws and chill.

Mix the remaining ingredients together and chill.

Serve the sauce with the chilled stone crab claws.

Serves four to six

———

There were four kinds of currency in the 1704 Connecticut colony: "pay" was barter at prices decided by annual vote; "money" was wampum or metallic money; "pay as money" was property at rates decided by the parties; "trust" was a price with time given. Money used in larger payments was mainly Spanish pieces worth about a dollar.

14

CRAB CAKES

2 lb. fresh Maryland blue crab meat	7 Ritz crackers, crushed
Olive oil for sautéing	1½ t. lemon juice
⅔ C. mayonnaise	½ t. white pepper
2 t. Worcestershire sauce	1 t. Tabasco pepper sauce
1½ t. dry mustard	⅓ C. unflavored bread crumbs
1 t. salt	1 extra-large egg
2 T. chopped parsley	Lemon wedges for garnish

Mix everything *except the crab meat and the olive oil* in a large bowl.

After all of the ingredients are mixed, gently fold in the crab meat.

Form the mixture into 5 to 6 ounce cakes.

Sauté in the olive oil over medium heat for approximately 3 minutes on each side.

Garnish with lemon wedges. (Tartar or cocktail sauce is optional.)

Serve with rice pilaf and a green vegetable or coleslaw.

Serves four to six

KEY LIME PIE

3 large egg whites
4 large egg yolks
5 oz. sweetened
condensed milk

5 oz. key lime juice
9" graham cracker pie
shell

Pre-heat the oven to 350°.

Beat the egg whites to soft peaks and reserve.

Beat the egg yolks for 3 to 5 minutes until smooth.

Slowly beat in the condensed milk.

Beat in the lime juice.

Gently fold in the egg whites.

Place the mixture in the pie shell.

Bake in the pre-heated 350° oven for 25 to 30 minutes.

Serves six

The Reverend Thomas Hooker is considered the "father of Connecticut".

16

PARADISE BAR & GRILL
78 Southfield Ave., Stamford
(203) 323-1116

Paradise Bar & Grill is tucked at the edge of Stamford Landing, a gleaming complex of office buildings and high-rise condos located on Stamford Harbor. Owner Klaus Schmidt was involved with the Landing's developer and the building that is home to *Paradise Bar & Grill* was the last constructed; Klaus's own dream come true.

Once through the door, patrons, families as well as the business people who flock here for lunch, dinner or just to loosen up, will wonder if they're still in Stamford: *Paradise Bar & Grill* exudes a tropical Caribbean exuberance that is reflected in the menu and music, as well as with each sip of one of its frozen drinks. During the summer, the floor to ceiling windows disappear, literally bringing the outdoors indoors.

The menu changes every six months; past offerings have ranged from Smoked Trout to Cape Cobb Salad to Lamb Stew. But Chef Jimmy Myers says he has a special appreciation for creating fish entrees.

Klaus says, "The Caribbean atmosphere has always thrilled me," and he trusts it will thrill patrons as well at *Paradise Bar & Grill*.

CALIFORNIA CRUNCHES

Loaf of French bread,
cut into ½" slices
½ C. olive oil plus extra
for vegetables
2 T. chopped fresh garlic
2 T. chopped fresh
parsley
Salt and pepper to taste
5 round eggplant slices
1 large portabello
mushroom cap, sliced
1 green squash, sliced

lengthwise
1 yellow squash, sliced
lengthwise
1 large roasted red
pepper
2 C. diced fresh tomatoes
¼ C. balsamic vinegar
2 T. chopped fresh basil
1 t. dried oregano
2 large balls of fresh
mozzarella cheese

Combine ¼ cup of the olive oil with the garlic,
parsley, salt, and pepper. Brush the bread slices
with the mixture. Bake at 400° until light brown.

Mix the diced tomatoes with the remaining olive
oil, balsamic vinegar, basil, oregano, salt and
pepper; let stand for 1 hour. Brush the vegetables
with some oil and grill until soft.

Cut the grilled vegetables into 1" pieces and
arrange on top of the French bread toasts. Top
with thin slices of mozzarella and bake until cheese
is melted. Top with cool tomato salad and serve
immediately.

Makes fifteen to twenty crunches

PARADISE SMOKED SALMON SANDWICH

½ lb. Atlantic sliced smoked salmon
6 pieces pumpernickel bread
½ C. herb cream cheese

1 cucumber, sliced into 18 pieces
1 C. shredded carrots
1 C. thinly sliced red onion
½ C. capers, non-pareil

Toast the pumperknickel bread and spread with the herb cream cheese.

Cut each slice into 3 pieces.

Top with a cucumber slice, smoked salmon, carrots, onions, and capers.

Serve with good pickles and your favorite salad.

Serves four

Paradise Bar & Grill's recipes were created by Chef Jimmy Myers

RED SNAPPER WITH SUN DRIED TOMATOES, BASIL AND PINENUTS

4 (8 oz.) red snapper filets, bones and skin removed
½ C. flour
Salt and pepper to taste
¼ C. olive oil
½ stick unsalted butter
1 T. chopped shallots

½ C. dry white wine
8 oz. jar clam juice
½ C. shredded fresh basil
1 C. sliced sun dried tomatoes
½ C. toasted pinenuts

Dip the red snapper filets into flour seasoned with salt and pepper. Shake off the excess.

In a hot skillet, add the olive oil and ¼ stick of the butter. Sauté both sides of the snapper until it is golden brown.

Transfer the fish to a cookie sheet and place in a warm oven.

Pour out the pan juices and add the shallots and white wine. Reduce by half.

Add the clam juice, basil, sun dried tomatoes, and pinenuts. Reduce by a third.

Stir in the remaining butter and season with salt and pepper. Serve snapper topped with sauce, rice pilaf and seasonal vegetables.

Serves four

Norwalk

First in recorded history came a navigator, Adriaen Block, in 1614 who called Norwalk Islands "Archipelago". In 1640, Daniel Patrick from the New Haven Colony obtained a deed from local Indians conveying land on the west side of the Norwalk River. But that colony sent no settlers to the grant. Roger Ludlow of the Connecticut Colony, perhaps to halt further penetration by Patrick's claim towards his Fairfield settlement, secured an Indian grant of land on the east side of the river in 1641. Neither Patrick nor Ludlow settled here. In 1651 Nathaniel Ely and Richard Olmstead led thirteen families from the Hartford area to the Ludlow grant.

The first homes rose on both sides of a path, now East Avenue near its intersection with Fort Point Street. On September 22, 1651, the General Court of the Connecticut Colony decreed "that Norwauke shall bee a Towne".

THE RESTAURANT at Rowyaton Seafood
89 Rowayton Ave., Rowayton
(203) 866-4488

Blue point oysters, also known as 'Connecticut candies', are one of the mainstays on the menu at the *Restaurant at Rowayton Seafood*. But blue points are only one of the many different types of oysters available at this eatery tucked among the boats on Rowayton Avenue.

Situated on the Five Mile River, boaters are only a quick '1/2 mile' to Long Island Sound. During the summer, diners can watch as many as 700 sail boats maneuver the coastal waters.

Rowayton, a section of Norwalk, has long been a seafaring and oystering community. *The Restaurant* is in a neighborhood of 100 year old houses and is itself located in the old Captain Henry House. In the early 1900s, it was a reading room.

The Restaurant at Rowayton Seafood serves "good traditional seafood, fresh from its affiliated seafood market, grilled, chilled, broiled or fried". The food is served in a casual atmosphere where the sunlight shining through the many windows makes the hardwood floors shimmer. Meanwhile, the sounds of boats signal their presence and passage.

SESAME SEARED TUNA
WITH SHOYU GLAZE AND WASABI SAUCE

2 (6 oz.) portions of
Grade A tuna
2 T. black sesame seeds

2 T. white sesame seeds
Salt and pepper
Griddle or sauté pan

Combine the black and white sesame seeds in a small bowl; season the tuna with a little salt and pepper. Roll the tuna in the sesame seeds until all sides are covered.

Heat the griddle or sauté pan until it is *very hot. Do not use any oil: The use of oil here will fry the seeds instantly and give the tuna an unwanted flavor.*

Place tuna in a hot pan and when the white seeds begin to brown, turn the tuna over to the next side. This may take only 1 minute or less on each side!

When all sides have been seared, remove the tuna from the pan and with the sharpest, thinnest knife you have, slice the tuna into 4 or 5 pieces.

Serve with a good amount of Shoyu Glaze and a touch of Wasabi Sauce. For those who find the Wasabi Sauce too spicy, try the Lemon Wasabi Mayonnaise for a creamier flavor with a touch of picante. *(recipes follow)*

Serves two

SHOYU GLAZE

2 C. good quality orange juice
1 T. chopped fresh ginger

1 T. dark brown sugar
¼ C. Kikkoman soy sauce

Reduce the orange juice and ginger together in a small sauce pan until the juice becomes thick.

Whisk in the brown sugar and the soy sauce; bring the mixture back to a boil. Taste to see if it has a nice balance of sweet, sour, fruit, and ginger flavor. Adjust the sauce if needed, then strain through a fine strainer and cool.

WASABI SAUCE

2 C. wasabi powder
1 C. rice wine vinegar

Water

In a mixing bowl, slowly add the rice wine vinegar and enough water to the wasabi powder until it reaches a sauce consistency.

This is a *very* powerful sauce so it should be used very lightly on fish.

Use about 1 part of Wasabi Sauce to 5 parts Shoyu Glaze for a nice balance of flavor.

MARYLAND LUMP CRAB CAKES
WITH LEMON WASABI MAYONNAISE

1 lb. Maryland lump crab	1 T. Old Bay Seasoning
1 C. bread crumbs	½ C. butter, melted
¼ C. chopped parsley	1 t. salt
Juice from 2 lemons	1 t. pepper

Pick through the crab meat to remove shells, then mix all of the ingredients together.

Form the mixture into 2 (3 oz. each) cakes.

Sear the cakes in a either a dry hot pan or a pan with a little butter, for 2 minutes on each side.

Serve with the Lemon Wasabi Mayonnaise.

LEMON WASABI MAYONNAISE

1 C. mayonnaise	1 T. lemon juice
1 t. wasabi powder	1 t. prepared horseradish

In a small mixing bowl, combine all of the ingredients.

Taste and adjust the flavor with wasabi powder, depending on how hot you like your sauce.

SONO SEAPORT SEAFOOD
100 Water St., Norwalk
(203) 854-9483

People who remember the South Norwalk of the 1930s and 1940s may remember when 100 Water Street was a booming oyster yard. The sounds of boats and sailors still trill the air, but *Sono Seaport Seafood* is now the beacon drawing crowds to the site.

It all began in 1983 with the opening of the Sono Seafood Market followed two years later by the restaurant. The full service family-oriented restaurant with its outdoor raw bar housed in a replica of a lighthouse, serves fresh seafood with the lobsters brought in right from the sea by Sono's own fishing boats. The chef notes that the oysters come directly from nearby Talmadge Brothers, another South Norwalk landmark.

Every seat in the house has a view of Norwalk Harbor. While diners gazing out at the horizon haven't reported seeing any dolphins, they do keep their eyes open for the tugboats, tankers, and, of course, the pleasure boats and yachts that cruise the Sound.

At *Sono Seaport Seafood,* every diner will find the atmosphere as welcoming as the seasonal seafood offerings are tasty.

JAMBALAYA

1 lb. andouille sausage	½ onion, chopped
½ lb. smoked ham	3 scallions, chopped
2 T. butter	1 jalepeño, chopped
4 T. flour	1 T. crushed garlic
¾ C. tomato juice	Shake of cumin
½ C. dark beer	Shake of allspice
3 large tomatoes, peeled	Shake cayenne pepper
and chopped	2 shakes of thyme
½ green pepper, chopped	1¼ C. tomato paste
½ red pepper, chopped	Soft shell crabs, shrimp,
1 celery stalk, chopped	and chicken, cooked
1 carrot, chopped	separately in butter

In a large pot on medium heat, make a roux by melting the butter and then adding the flour. Sir continuously until the roux is blonde.

Stir in the tomato juice and the beer, whisking the mixture until it simmers. Add the sausage and ham and cook on medium heat for 10 to 15 minutes.

Mix in the remaining ingredients *except the seafood and chicken,* and continue to cook on medium heat for about 15 minutes longer.

Add the cooked seafood and chicken to the base and serve together over white rice.

Serves six

27

MUSSELS FRA DIABLO

50 mussels, scrubbed and de-bearded
2 T. oil
1 medium onion, diced
1 C. green peppers, chopped
1 garlic clove, chopped
24 oz. crushed tomatoes
1½ C. tomato sauce
½ C. white wine
1 C. chopped fresh parsley
Salt and pepper to taste
½ C. Parmesan cheese
2 T. sugar
2 bay leaves
Optional: Consider adding other seafoods to the pot, especially shrimp.
Cooked linguini

Add the oil to a large pot and sauté the onions, green peppers, and garlic.

Stir in the crushed tomatoes and the tomato sauce.

Add all of the remaining ingredients *except the mussels, other seafood, and cooked linguini.*

Bring the pot to a simmer and cook for about 30 minutes.

Add the mussels to the pot, reduce the heat to low and steam the mussels for 3 to 4 minutes.

Remove the bay leaves before serving over linguini.

Serves six

HURRICANE'S
80 Seaview Avenue, Norwalk
(203) 852-1257

Pulling up to *Hurricane's* for the first time, patrons might be puzzled a bit by the building's appearance. It looks familiar, but why?

The why is because not many restaurants are housed in Quonset huts.

This building has seen many lives. According to owners Andy Maciel and Mike Brennan, it was first used as an army barracks in World War I. Then, in the 1930s, it was transformed into a penny arcade at Rowayton Point. To get it ready for its next incarnation, it was loaded onto a barge and floated to its present location where today regulars can drink or eat at the copper topped bar counter, shoot pool or join the dart league.

Diners can choose either the dining room that extends off the bar toward the water or pass through to the deck and listen to the boats languidly bob and sway.

Sitting at the bar, it is not difficult to feel as if you just finished a hard day's work at sea and now it's time to enjoy yourself at *Hurricane's*.

That sounds like a nice way to end a day.

BEER BATTER COCONUT SHRIMP

10 large shrimp, peeled
and deveined
2 eggs
2 C. Bisquick powder mix

1 can of beer
Shredded coconut
Oil for frying
Sweet and sour sauce

Mix the eggs into the Bisquick. Using a whisk, slowly add the beer, constantly whisking the mixture.

Continue adding beer until the batter is thick enough so that it barely drips off a shrimp.

After the batter has been tested for proper consistency, add the amount of shredded coconut that suits your taste and mix well.

Dip the shrimp into the batter and quickly fry in a pan. Remove and serve with the sweet and sour sauce.

Serves four

Bean-porridge, a soup made of salt meat, beans, and seasoned with herbs, was a common breakfast for colonial farmers.

SEAFOOD BISQUE

Butter for sautéing
1 C. scallops
1 C. chopped shrimp *or*
canned tiny shrimp
1 onion, chopped
1 celery stalk, chopped
1 T. garlic, chopped
1 T. black pepper

1 T. basil
1 C. white wine
1 C. clam juice
1 C. cream
Roux: About 2 T. oil
mixed with enough flour
to make a thin paste

Heat the butter in a large pan.

Sauté the chopped onions, celery, and garlic.

Add the black pepper and basil.

When the onions are opaque, add the white wine, scallops, and shrimp.

Simmer for a few minutes, than add the clam juice and next the cream. Stir.

Sir in the roux. The roux will cause the soup to thicken.

Continue to simmer until the bisque has thickened to a creamy consistency.

Serves six

MARISCO PICANTI
Spicy Portuguese Seafood

12 shrimp, peeled and
deveined
1 C. bay scallops
1 C. sliced calamari
½ stick butter
1 link chorizo sausage,
sliced
1 T. crushed garlic

½ onion, chopped
1 T. Cajun seasoning
1 T. basil
1 t. black pepper
1 C. wine
½ C. tomato puree
Cooked wild rice

Place the butter in a frying pan and melt it on medium heat.

Add the sliced chorizo, garlic, onions, Cajun seasoning, basil, and black pepper.

When the onions start to turn opaque, add the wine and the tomato puree.

Stir and simmer for about 10 minutes.

Add the shrimp first, then the scallops and finally the calamari, stirring as each seafood is added.

When the calamari is cooked, serve spooned over wild rice.

Serves four

Westport

For nearly two hundred years after the first white settlement here in 1648, the area east of the Saugatuck River belonged to the West Parish of Fairfield, that west of the river to the Town of Norwalk. Before the Revolution the river had become a commercial route and by the early 19th century the village, then known as Saugatuck, was a thriving port for regional produce and goods. This prompted Daniel Nash and others in 1835 to secure the incorporation of Westport from parts of Norwalk, Fairfield, and Weston. The Battle of Compo Hill was its contribution to the Revolution when, on April 25, 1777, patriots engaged British troops in a sharp skirmish. In the 1840's the population was augmented by Irish and later by Italian workers who built the railroad and settled in the present village of Saugatuck. Before World War I, noted artists and writers began living here. Light industry and farming later yielded to urban pressures and by 1950 Westport had become primarily a residential suburban community.

BLACK DUCK CAFE
605 Riverside Ave., Westport
(203) 227-7978

The *Black Duck Cafe* has a bar that runs the length of this restaurant with windows that look out over the Saugatuck River with the Sound just a bit beyond.

Owner Peter Aitkin says that this establishment, which he has owned since 1978, is "more properly described as a bar and grill" or given the building's history, a "waterfront barge and grill".

The building is actually a former sea-going refrigeration and ice storage barge that was built around 1840. It has been anchored in Westport since 1961. The restaurant is named after a legendary rum-running boat. The menu is presented as a newsletter and it provides the rest of the story. Peter himself was once an off-shore power boat racer but his nautical adventures are more relaxed nowadays.

The *Black Duck Cafe*, which has a varied menu, is best known for its hamburgers. Peter says his place is a "blue collar bar in a white collar town" where families, bikers, and stock-brokers all enjoy the eclectic ambiance. At night, especially on weekends, the *Cafe* really comes alive.

BUFFALO WINGS

HOT WING SAUCE

2 T. margarine
3 T. clover honey
1½ t. light brown sugar
¾ T. chili powder

Few drops of Tabasco
pepper sauce
1 C. Durkee red hot sauce

Combine all ingredients *except red hot sauce* in a
sauce pan. Heat until melted; mix well. Add the red
hot sauce and whisk until everything is well blended.

Yields one cup

BUFFALO WINGS

12 chicken wings, split
Oil for frying
7 carrot sticks
7 celery sticks

¼ C. blue cheese dressing
Green lettuce leaf
¼ C. Hot Wing Sauce

Deep fry the wings for required amount of time,
about 1½ minutes after they begin to float.

While the chicken is cooking, set a plate with the
lettuce leaf at one end and put some blue cheese
dressing on it. Arrange the celery and carrot sticks
alongside. Dip the chicken wings in the hot sauce
and place them on the plate.

Serves four

STEAMERS

3 lbs. steamers
1½ T. chopped garlic
1 T. dried basil

1 T. oregano
1 C. white wine
¼ C. butter, melted

Put the steamers, garlic, basil, oregano, and white wine in a pot.

Simmer until the clams open.

Serve with the broth and melted butter.

Serves two

The Eleven Articles known as the Fundamental Orders was the first written constitution in America but there is no evidence it was ever adopted by a direct vote of the people. One of Connecticut's nicknames is the Constitution State.

CHICKEN MARSALA

1 (5 oz.) boneless chicken
breast
Flour for dredging
4 T. butter
3 oz. marsala wine
Basil to taste

Oregano to taste
½ C. fresh mushrooms,
sliced
Salt and pepper, to taste
Cooked linguini

Dredge the chicken breast in the flour.

Melt the butter in a pan and sauté the chicken until
it is almost cooked, about 4½ minutes on each side.

Add the wine, basil, oregano, mushrooms, and salt
and pepper.

Simmer for 5 minutes.

Serve on a bed of linguini.

Serves one

───────────────

Some believe that the lean-to house, or salt-box style, was adopted to avoid paying an extra colonial tax.

SPLASH PACIFIC RIM GRILL
260 South Compo Rd., Westport
(203) 454-7798

The *Splash Pacific Rim Grill* is at the end of the half mile driveway through the public golf course at Longshore. If you haven't been there recently, you're in for a surprise.

The restaurant is no longer a traditional New England seafood establishment thought of primarily during the summer. Instead, it has been reincarnated as a dining destination serving the cuisines of the Pacific rim. At *Splash*, portions are designed to be shared and served family style and patrons are encouraged to ask the server for help in ordering.

The interior is true to its aquatic location on Long Island Sound: a mosaic 'wave' forms an interior wall and even the bar has an undulating shape. The dishes were chosen for their resemblance to sea glass. And at night, tiny lights disbursed within the 'wave' make the room twinkle, creating an impression of being under the sea.

There is an outside bar, tiki torches, and teak deck furniture. *Splash's* goal is to "present inspired cuisine in an equally inspired ambience" — a choice for diners looking for a sophisticated, yet casual, adult dining experience.

SPANISH CLAM CHOWDER

1 lb. frozen clams, chopped, liquid reserved
4 slices slab bacon, diced
1 medium onion, chopped fine
1 leek, sliced and washed
2 scallions, minced
2 stalks celery, diced
1 red pepper, diced
4 T. Thai yellow curry*
4 T. all-purpose flour
2 qts. clam juice
12 oz. purple potatoes, peeled and diced

1 bay leaf
1 t. thyme
Salt and black pepper, to taste
1 pt. heavy cream
Garnish: Thinly sliced scallion greens and toasted sourdough bread
*Available in specialty markets or Asian section of grocer. Can substitute any other Thai curry or omit altogether. Thai curry adds a spicy depth.

In a heavy bottomed sauce pot, cook the bacon until it is lightly browned. Remove and reserve.

Add the onions and leeks to the pot and sauté on low heat until soft.

Add the scallions, celery, and red peppers.

Sauté 1 minute.

Add the curry paste and sprinkle with flour, stir to coat well.

Whisk in clam juice. *(Continued...)*

Stir over medium heat until the mixture comes to a boil.

Turn to low simmer.

Add the potatoes, bay leaf, and thyme.

Season with salt and pepper to taste.

Stir in cream and simmer until potatoes are tender.

Stir in the clams and cook for an additional few minutes. Remove the bay leaf.

Garnish with thinly sliced scallion greens and toasted sourdough bread.

Serve immediately.

Yields about four quarts of soup

William and Mary granted the colonies the right to have a postal system, and the first regular mounted post from New York to Boston started on January 1, 1684.

BBQ SALMON SAUCE

½ C. honey
¼ C. brown sugar
2 T. miso paste
1 T. molasses
2¼ T. soy sauce
1 T. plum wine
1 T. Japanese mustard
1 T. minced fresh ginger
2 scallions

2 T. sesame oil
¾ C. peanut oil
1 T. rice vinegar
Salmon steaks
Bok choy
Fresh spinach
Radicchio
Fresh cilantro

Whisk together the honey, brown sugar, miso paste, molasses, soy sauce, plum wine, and Japanese mustard.

In a blender, puree the ginger, scallions, sesame oil, peanut oil, and rice vinegar.

Whisk all of the ingredients together.

Grill the salmon steaks, paint with the BBQ sauce.

Stir fry the bok choy, spinach, and radicchio.

Mound the greens in the center of a plate and top with the salmon. Garnish with the cilantro.

Serves four

GINGER COCONUT RICE

2 T. peanut oil
2 garlic cloves, minced
½ medium onion, minced
1½ C. jasmine rice
1 C. coconut milk

1½ C. water
2 T. minced ginger
Salt and pepper, to taste
Garnish: minced pickled
ginger

Sauté the garlic and onions in the oil in a pot until the onions are soft.

Add the rice, coconut milk, water, ginger, salt and pepper.

Simmer for 15 minutes in a covered pot.

Turn off the heat and let the pot sit for 15 minutes.

Garnish with the pickled ginger and serve.

Serves four to six

_Splash's recipes were
created by Chef Peter Klein_

SABBIA RISTORANTE MEDITERRANEO
233 Hillspoint Rd., Westport
(203) 454-4922

Jeff Abate, a Culinary Institute of America graduate and the former chef at Sole in New Canaan and Terra in Greenwich, has brought his exceptional culinary skills to the newest addition to Westport's coast, *Sabbia Ristorante*, according to general manager, Cesare Sforza. *Sabbia* is where Cafe de la Plage reigned for more than a quarter of a century; *Sabbia* has brought a new vision to the spot. The building has been completely renovated and no detail has been over-looked by owner Gaitano Iovieno (who also owns two other Westport restaurants). This casually elegant bistro serving northern Italian cuisine with a French twist, has cherry wood chairs and tables made in Italy; honed limestone and onyx floor tiles interspersed with Alchamey glass and fossil tiles; and the restroom boasts a burnished fossil sink an French limestone counters.

Cesare says that *Sabbia* is "on the edge in Westport" and they strive to create a special magic. A special touch is the complementary after-dinner glass of limoncello, a drink that goes perfectly with the not to be forgotten water views. Cesare says that "between the menu and the look, *Sabbia* is a total magical package."

GRILLED SALMON IN OYSTER MUSHROOM CREAM SAUCE, ROASTED POTATOES, AND ARUGULA SALAD

4 (7 oz. each) salmon filets
12 red bliss potatoes
Olive oil to coat potatoes and salmon
2 sprigs rosemary, trimmed and chopped
Salt and pepper, to taste
4 sliced shallots

3 C. cleaned oyster mushrooms
1 C. white wine
3 C. heavy cream
1 bunch aruugla, washed
½ C. lemon juice
½ C. olive oil

Cut the potatoes into quarters and roast them on a pan at 400° with oil, rosemary, and salt and pepper, until golden brown.

Sauté the shallots in a pan until translucent; add the mushrooms and season. When they are reduced, add the wine, cook until dry, then add the cream and simmer for 10 minutes.

In a blender, blend the lemon juice, slowing add the oil to emulsify. Season and toss with the arugula.

Season the salmon on both sides and coat with oil. Grill until medium rare.

Divide the potatoes onto four plates, top with the salmon; top with the sauce. Serve with the arugula salad and lemon vinaigrette.

Serves four

ARUGULA AND RADICCHIO SALAD WITH GORGONZOLA AND WARM FIG, PORT DRESSING

½ C. port
1 T. sugar
6 oz. dried figs, without stems
¼ C. balsamic vinegar
2 medium shallots
½ C. extra virgin olive oil
Salt and pepper to taste

2 large bunches arugula, washed
1 head radicchio, washed and cut into bite size pieces
¼ lb. Gorgonzola cheese, crumbled

In a sauce pan, bring first four ingredients to a boil.

Simmer until the figs are soft, about 15 minutes. Remove half of the figs and, when they are cool, cut them into small peices. Set aside.

Put the fig-port mixture and the shallots into a blender and begin to process. While processing, drizzle in the olive oil to form an emulsion. When finished, add the fig pieces back in.

When ready to serve, re-warm the dressing. Season with salt and pepper; toss the arugula and radicchio with the dressing. Top with the Gorgonzola cheese.

Serves six

Sabbia's recipes were created by Chef Jeff Abate

45

LEMON TART

12" pastry tart shell	5 oz. butter
Juice of 2 lemons	2 C. sugar
6 eggs	Zest of 3 lemons

Pre-heat oven at 400°.

In a bowl over a simmering pot of water, whisk together the lemon juice, eggs, butter, and sugar for about 15 minutes or until thick.

Strain through a sieve.

Add the zest. Pour into tart shell and bake at 400° for 5 minutes. Cool slightly before serving or serve cold.

Consider serving with fresh berries.

A superstitious people, the Puritans determined their crop planting times according to the phases of the moon: potatoes, carrots, and beets, growing underground, were planted in the "dark of the moon"; corn, peas, and beans were planted in the "light of the moon".

ALLEN'S CLAM & LOBSTER HOUSE*
191 Hillspoint Rd., Westport
(203) 226-4411

If *Allen's Clam & Lobster House* could talk,
it would have quite a tale to tell. Located directly
on Sherwood Mill Pond with Long Island Sound
just beyond, the building was originally Nash's
Oyster House. The structure was built using
salvage from sailing vessels that ran aground at
the turn of the century. (If you look carefully,
you'll be able to spy some old ship knees serving
as structural supports.) In 1909, Captain Allen
married a Nash daughter and they changed the
name to Allen's. They operated the business for a
few decades.

Meanwhile, present owners Ron and
Wayne Uccenelli's grandfather became the first
plumber in Westport. But his true love was
running clambakes for civic groups in the area.
He always bought his seafood from Captain
Allen and in 1958, after Captain Allen's death,
he bought the business, retaining the name.

Today the grandsons continue the
tradition set by their patriarch. Ron describes
Allen's as a "rustic New England seafood
restaurant: traditional, the way things used to
be." (*Allen's East at 60 Beach Road in Lordship,
Stratford, also has water views.*)

COLESLAW DRESSING

2 C. mayonnaise
¼ C. fresh parsley,
chopped
¼ large red onion, minced
2½ t. lemon juice
¼ C. sugar
1 t. black pepper

¼ t. celery salt
3 T. Dijon mustard
Dash Worcestershire
sauce
1½ T. red wine vinegar
1 T. horseradish
Coleslaw

Mix all of the ingredients, except the coleslaw, together.

Toss the dressing with the coleslaw and serve.

Yields about one pint of dressing

The original grantees of the Connecticut Colony were the Puritans, or Non-conformists, who while they believed in the Church of England, believed it needed to be "purified" to eliminate remaining rituals and traditions of the Catholic Church.

48

MANHATTAN CHOWDER

16 whole quahog clams, slightly steamed and chopped
1 C. diced salt pork
½ C. corn oil
3 onions, diced
½ celery stalk, diced
4 large carrots, diced
1 T. dry mustard
1 T. chopped parsley, fresh or dried
½ T. oregano
½ T. thyme
3 bay leaves
½ T. black pepper
Pinch cayenne pepper
½ t. poultry seasoning
2 dashes of Worcestershire sauce
Dash Tabasco pepper sauce
½ T. chopped garlic
6 C. clam juice
29 oz. can of potatoes, drained and diced
29 oz. can tomatoes with puree
1 T. clam base *(optional)*

Sauté the salt pork in a soup pot; remove pork once fat has been rendered. Add corn oil, onions, celery, and carrots; sauté until soft. Add spices and garlic. Sauté 2 to 3 minutes.

In another pot, heat clam juice, clam base, and potatoes.

Stir the tomatoes into the onion mixture; cook on medium heat for 5 minutes. Once the clam broth is hot, mix it in with the onions and tomatoes. Simmer for 20 minutes. Add the clams and simmer for 10 minutes longer. Remove the bay leaves.

Serves six to eight

49

SHELLFISH DIANE

8 large shrimp, peeled
and deveined
1½ lb. sea scallops
4 lobster tails, sliced in
half, plus 8 claws *(pre-
cooked)*
1 C. sliced mushrooms
2 T. olive oil
4 whole garlic cloves

4 scallions, white part
only, sliced
8 sun-dried tomato slices
1 T. fresh chopped
parsley
1 T. fresh chopped basil
Salt and pepper to taste
¼ C. white wine
Cooked pasta

Sauté all of the ingredients, *except the wine and
pasta,* in the oil on medium high for about 3
minutes or until the scallops and shrimp are cooked.

If using a gas stove, turn the heat to high and add
the wine and carefully flambé.

If using an electric stove, add the wine and turn
off the stove.

Serve over cooked pasta.

Serves four

---

*Hasty pudding is a boiled meal of corn or
rye sweetened with molasses or maple syrup.*

50

Bridgeport
"The Park City"

The area that is now Bridgeport was settled in the mid-17th century by farmers from the older towns of Stratford and Fairfield. Centers of settlement were Stratfield, present North Avenue; Pembroke, now Old Mill Green; and Newfield, present downtown. The site of Bridgeport was owned by the Pequonnock or Golden Hill band of the Paugussett Indian tribe. In 1695, the settlers of the area established a church, Pequonnock Parish. Newfield was renamed Bridgeport and made a borough of the Town of Stratford in 1800.

Bridgeport became an independent town in 1821, and in 1836 was chartered as a city. Municipal bonds helped bring the Housatonic Railroad to Bridgeport. The city's success was due to its location on a good harbor and favorable railroad connections. With the introduction of steam power, harbor commerce was supplanted by manufacturing as the mainstay of the economy.

Bridgeport was made the county seat of Fairfield County in 1853. By the end of the Civil War, a thriving sewing machine industry had developed.

Bridgeport was the birthplace of the midget Tom Thumb, the residence of showman Phineas Taylor Barnum, and the home of his circus winter quarters. Immigrants from many states and countries settled here, found work, built homes and raised families.

Manufacturing in this heavily industrialized city aided the Allied cause during two world wars. From 1933 to 1957, local politics were dominated by the Socialist mayor, Jasper McLevy. Large areas of the city underwent urban renewal in the 1960s.

Since 1974 the largest city in Connecticut, Bridgeport today is part of the New York metropolitan area, yet remains a city of homes and neighborhoods.

BLOODROOT

85 Ferris St., Bridgeport
(203) 576-9168

The menu at *Bloodroot*, the feminist
vegetarian restaurant located in a former home
on Burr Creek in Black Rock, changes
seasonally, with selections reflecting the bounty
harvested from the collective's garden. The novel
offerings with their international influences
challenge preconceptions about vegetarianism.

Bloodroot is a feminist collective whose
members believe "everything people do is
political".

Selma Miriam believes humans shouldn't
add to the depletion of the earth's resources and
should instead live lightly on the earth. As
feminists they support the rights of all living
beings, including animals, and many of the
recipes are now non-dairy.

Bloodroot provides a library and bookstore
for browsing; an atmosphere conducive to
discourse; and periodically presents speakers; all
in addition to its delectable food.

Bloodroot Vegetarian Restaurant is a
relaxing eclectic self-serve restaurant that defies
definition — it must be experienced to be
appreciated.

BEET AND ORANGE SALAD

4 fresh beets
½ C. water
2 T. lemon juice
2 T. orange juice
¼ C. olive oil
Grated rind of half an orange
½ t. salt
2 oranges, peeled and sliced
Hot pepper flakes

¼ C. pepitas *(squash seeds, available in health food stores; whole fennel or caraway seeds can be used the same way)*
Lettuce leaves
Escarole hearts
Watercress leaves
Optional: Green pepper slices and Portuguese olives

Scrape the beets to remove the hairs and dirt. Rinse the knife, but *don't* wash the beets.

Slice the beets and place them in a wide-bottomed pot. Add the water, cover, and cook over moderate heat until just tender. Cool, chill.

Make the dressing by mixing together the lemon juice, orange juice, olive oil, and orange rind. Add the salt, stir well and set aside.

Place the orange slices in a dish and sprinkle them lightly with a few hot pepper flakes.

Pan roast the pepitas by shaking them in a small frying pan over high heat until light brown.

(Continued...)

When cool, crush in a processor or with a mortar and pestle.

To compose the salad, make a bed of greens using lettuce, escarole hearts, and watercress.

Arrange the beet and orange slices on top, adding the green pepper slices and Portuguese olives, if desired.

Pour the dressing over the salad and sprinkle generously with the ground pepitas.

Serves six

From *Perennial Political Palate* by the Bloodroot Collective, Sanguinaria Publishing

SPANISH LENTIL AND GARLIC SOUP

2½ C. green lentils
Water for soaking
4 C. Swiss chard,
shredded and packed
2 large red peppers, diced
2½ C. potatoes, peeled
and diced
2 C. diced carrots

1 large tomato, diced
Whole head of garlic,
peeled
2-3 bay leaves
½ C. olive oil
12 C. water
1 T. salt

Soak the lentils in water to cover for 3 hours, or until they have softened and are swollen. *(Note: the soaking and cooking times are very important.)*

Drain the lentils and turn into a big soup pot. Add all of the ingredients, except the salt, and bring the soup to a boil.

Turn the flame down and simmer for 2 to 3 hours, or until the lentils have virtually dissolved.

Add the salt and simmer a few minutes longer.

More salt or water may be needed.

Remove the bay leaves.

Serves ten to twelve

PUMPKIN TOFU CUSTARD

1½ C. steamed pumpkin
or Hubbard squash
1 lb. tofu
⅔ C. maple syrup
⅞ C. water
⅓ C. oil
¾ t. salt
⅔ t. cinnamon

⅔ t. ginger
¼ t. nutmeg
Scant t. vanilla
Dash of cloves
½ C. unsweetened dried
coconut
½ C. very hot tap water

Put the pumpkin or squash into a blender or processor together with the tofu, maple syrup, water, and oil. Add salt, cinnamon, ginger, nutmeg, vanilla, and cloves and blend until smooth.

Turn the mixture into custard cups and place in a pan. Pour water into the pan to a depth of 1".

Bake at 375° until the custards darken and seem firm then remove from the pan and refrigerate.

Coconut Creme: Place coconut in a blender, add water and process. Strain, pressing down on the coconut to extract the liquid. Discard the coconut pulp and refrigerate the "creme". *(It is very perishable.)* Serve over custard.

Serves ten to twelve

CAPTAIN'S COVE SEAPORT
1 Bostwick Ave., Bridgeport
(203) 335-7104

Captain's Cove is a family oriented stop that is the realized dream of owner Kay Williams. He took an abandoned marina and, over many years, transformed it into an exciting nautical-themed entertainment and educational spot.

The whole Williams clan is involved in this enterprise which includes a restaurant offering everything from hot dogs and hamburgers to lobster bakes and a special fish and chips which they "fry themselves around the clock".

Captain's Cove is the home port of the internationally renowned H.M.S. Rose; fishing seminars are offered; there are historical tours of Black Rock Harbor; and a Maritime Museum recently opened. There is something different happening nearly every night such as music, country line dancing or games night.

The *Cove* is always evolving; each visit will uncover a new discovery. From the 43-foot long replica of the Titanic suspended over the tugboat bar to the little shops in Victorian pastel colors that line the boardwalk, Jill Williams' advice is to "Come, sit, relax, shop, take a boat ride, historic boat tour or eat. There's something for everyone." (Seasonal)

CLAMS CASINO

Little neck clams, the smaller the better
Italian flavored bread crumbs

Butter
Bacon, cut the strips into 1" squares

Shuck the clams and place on a foil lined sheet pan.

Make sure the clam is separated from the shell.

Discard the top half of the shell.

Sprinkle each clam with a ½ t. of the bread crumbs.

Place a small pat of butter on the bread crumbs.

Cover the whole clam with a piece of bacon.

Place the clams under the broiler and cook them until the bacon is done.

Remove from the oven and let them cool for a couple of minutes.

Captain's Cove's Jill Williams says, "I guarantee you'll be back shucking more clams when you finish these!"

LOBSTERMAN'S LOBSTER ROLL

2 (1 lb. each) lobsters, cooked, meat removed
½ C. mayonnaise
¼ C. chopped celery
2 T. chopped red onion

Juice from half a lemon
5 shakes of Tabasco pepper sauce (or to taste)
Hot dog rolls

Cut the lobster meat into chunks.

Put the lobster pieces into a bowl and add the mayonnaise, celery, onions, lemon juice, and pepper sauce. (Add more pepper sauce if you like it spicy.)

Mix and refrigerate for 1 hour or until cold.

Toast the hot dog rolls, fill, and enjoy.

Serves four

Connecticut began as two separate colonies: Connecticut Colony and New Haven Colony. The two became one in 1665.

60

DOLPHIN'S COVE
421 Seaview Ave., Bridgeport
(203) 335-3301

Dolphin's Cove, a Portuguese restaurant and nightclub that hugs Long Island Sound and is accessible by land or by sea, combines the historic old with the modern new.

The heart of the building, a 106 year old Victorian house, is the setting for the quiet dining area. The wood wainscoted walls, floors, and lace curtains that adorn the windows create a romantic, intimate ambiance. In contrast, the larger outer room, which features the bar, affords nautical views of the Sound and Bridgeport Harbor, with its pleasure boats, ships, barges and, of course, captain's view of the lighthouse. A new sport's bar recently opened upstairs.

Owner Jack Matias and his family bring a feeling of the Portuguese coast to Connecticut. A fishing family, the former owners of Golfinho's, a seafood market, still do their own lobstering. (Jack's nickname is Golfinho which is Portuguese for dolphin.)

Dolphin's Cove got some national attention, even mentioned in *Ranger Rick*, when a Florida manatee, the endangered mammal of mermaid lore, found its way to the restaurant's dock. So keep your eyes seaward!

SEAFOOD RAY

5 T. butter	3 large mushrooms, sliced
4 (6 oz.) lobster tails, split	½ C. Madeira wine
4 medium size shrimp,	2 T. cornstarch
peeled and de-veined	¼ C. water
8 bay scallops	1 lb. cooked pasta

Melt the butter in a large pan.

Add the lobster, shrimp, scallops, and mushrooms.

Sauté until just about cooked, then add the wine.

Simmer for 1 minute.

Mix the cornstarch with the water.

Add the cornstarch to the pan, blending well.

Once the sauce thickens, serve with the pasta.

Serves four

John Haynes was the Colony of Connecticut's first governor in 1639.

CLAMS PORTUGUESE

6 cherry stone clams, scrubbed
½ C. tomato sauce
2 sprigs of cilantro
1 T. chopped onions

3 bacon slices, chopped small
5 slices of good sausage
½ C. red wine
2 T. brandy

Put the tomato sauce in a pot.

Add the clams, cilantro, onions, bacon, sausage, and red wine to the tomato sauce.

Cook on medium heat.

Watch for the clams to steam open.

Once the clams open, add the brandy.

Serve immediately.

Serves one

The Dutch navigator Adrian Block is believed to be the first white man to voyage up the Connecticut River, which he named Freshwater.

FLAN

6 large eggs	Caramelized sugar*
6 T. sugar	*Bottles of caramelized*
6 C. milk	*sugar available in grocer's*
Zest of one orange	*Portuguese section or at*
2 T. brandy	*Portuguese markets*

Thoroughly mix together the eggs, sugar, milk, and orange zest.

Mix in the brandy.

Coat the bottom of an oven-safe (2 qt. or larger) cake pan with the carmelized sugar.

Pour flan mixture on top of the caramelized sugar.

Place the cake pan into a larger pan and add water to come half way up side of cake pan.

Bake at 375° for 1 hour to 1 hour and 15 minutes or until a toothpick inserted into the middle of the flan comes out clean.

Cool well before flipping the flan out onto a serving dish before serving.

Serves four

Stratford

"Mac's Harbor", traditional landing place of Stratford's First Settlers in the spring of 1639 under leadership of the Reverend Adam Blakeman

On the right, at the inner end of the harbor, stood the First Meeting House and burial ground, and across the harbor at the stone embankment was erected the first Tide Mill in this the village of Cupheag, in 1643 renamed Stratford after Stratford-on-Avon, England

KNAPP'S LANDING
520 Sniffens Lane, Stratford
(203) 378-5999

To get to *Knapp's Landing*, one drives down Sniffen's Lane, the road that bisects the Allied Signal plants. Just when you're sure you made a wrong turn, the bright *Knapp's Landing* sign greets you.

Knapp's Landing was named for owner Patricia Massey's father. Area residents will fondly remember Tomiko's, the restaurant that introduced the Stratford region to Japanese cuisine. Tomiko is Pat's mother. Now Tomiko's daughter is continuing the family tradition. The building has been completely remodeled to take advantage of its waterfront location with its expansive views of Smith Point. The restaurant is bright and airy.

While the smoking section doesn't look directly out on the water, there is a 'water view': a precisely detailed full-wall mural colorfully duplicates the actual marshland scene outside complete with local oystermen.

You may not get a chance to study the mural though because you'll probably be too busy enjoying the food at this casual, family friendly addition to the coast.

66

BASIL SEARED RED SNAPPER
WITH LOBSTER BUTTER

2 (4-6 oz.) snapper filets
Basil Butter
Lobster Butter

BASIL BUTTER

¼ C. butter   Basil, fresh chopped
1 t. lemon juice

Cream everything together.

LOBSTER BUTTER

1 lb. lobster, cooked,   ¼ lb. butter
reserve shells

Sauté the lobster meat *and shells* in the butter on
low heat until the butter turns red and the lobster
flavor has been extracted. Remove the shells and
dice the lobster meat.

Return the meat to the butter and chill.

RED SNAPPER

2 (4-6 oz.) snapper filets   Basil butter
Salt and pepper   Bread crumbs
Flour for dredging   Lobster butter

Lightly salt and pepper the snapper, then dredge
it in the flour.   *(Continued...)*

Smooth some of the basil butter liberally on top of the snapper.

Sprinkle with the bread crumbs.

In a non-stick oven-safe pan on medium heat, place the buttered side of the snapper down in the pan.

Cook for about 1 minute or until a golden crust has formed.

Finish the fish in a 350° oven until the fish is firm, about 8 minutes.

Remove from the oven and top with the lobster butter.

Serve immediately.

Serves two

Knapp's Landing's recipes were created by Chef James Bernier.

CHICKEN TUSCANY

1 chicken breast,
julienned and floured
Vegetable oil
3 cloves of garlic,
slivered
3 oz. lemon juice
3 oz. white wine
4-6 oz. chicken stock
1 tomato, diced
4 roasted pepperoncini

2 eggplant rounds,
breaded, fried and
julienned
10 strips of red roasted
pepper, julienned
1 T. whole butter
1 T. fresh basil
1 C. shredded Monteray
Jack cheese
Cooked rice

Add the garlic to a hot pan with a few drops of
vegetable oil.

Sauté until the garlic is lightly browned, then add
the chicken breast.

Deglaze with the lemon juice and white wine.

Add the chicken stock.

Add the tomatoes, pepperoncini, eggplant, and the
roasted peppers.

Let it reduce fully, then add the butter and basil.

Top with the cheese, melt and serve on rice.

Serves one

CHOCOLATE ISLAND DELIGHT

CAKE

1 C. cocoa powder
2 C. *boiling* water
2¾ C. all-purpose flour
2 t. baking soda
½ t. salt

½ t. baking powder
1 C. butter, softened
2½ C. sugar
4 whole large eggs
1½ t. vanilla

Mix the cocoa powder with the water, then set aside.
Cream the butter and sugar, then add the eggs and
vanilla to the creamed mixture. Sift the dry ingredients
together, add them to the creamed mixture; add the
cocoa powder and water. Place in a non-stick floured
cake pan and bake at 350° until a toothpick inserted
into the center is dry; about 1 hour.

FILLING AND LAYERING

4 ripe bananas, sliced
thin
1½ C. heavy cream
3 T. Myers dark rum

2 T. sugar
1 C. finely chopped
walnuts

Whip the cream with the rum and sugar.

SIMPLE SYRUP

1 C. water   ½ C. sugar   2 T. Myers rum

Simmer the water and sugar together for 10 minutes.
Remove from the heat and add the rum. *(Continued...)*

70

ASSEMBLY

After the cake is cooled, remove it from the pan and slice it into 3 or 4 thin layers. Place the bottom layer on a cake decorating pan and soak liberally with the simple syrup. Put a small amount of whipped cream on top, smoothing it out, leaving ¼" from outer edge of cake uncovered.

Sprinkle with walnuts, then cover the whipped cream with a single layer of the sliced bananas. Place the next layer of cake on top and repeat process.

Make sure each layer is moistened thoroughly with the simple syrup and pressed firmly onto the layer beneath.

FROSTING

| 6 egg yolks | ½ C. water | 1½ T. cocoa powder |
| 1 C. sugar | 1 lb. butter | dissolved in ¼ C. water |

Place egg yolks in mixer with whip on high. Place sugar and water in a sauce pan. Cook to soft ball stage. Cube butter. Whip in the sugar and water with the egg yolks. Incorporate butter cubes 1 at a time and add cocoa and water mixture. Let cool 10 minutes, then frost the cake.

SEASCAPE
14 Beach Dr., Stratford
(203) 375-2149

Seascape is an aptly descriptive name for this restaurant which gazes upon Long Island Sound from its location across from the sea wall in Lordship. So when new owner and chef Jack Hodes acquired the business he retained the well-known moniker — but he says everything else is "new and improved" and reflects his culinary and restaurant philosophies.

Trained in fast-paced Manhattan, Jack describes himself as laid-back and he wants diners to feel relaxed and comfortable while at *Seascape*. His resume includes Lipstick Cafe and Vong's, a French/Thai restaurant owned by famed chef/owner Jean-Georges Vongerichten, both in the City.

Jack's wife Traci's Connecticut roots brought them to the Nutmeg State where he says he is able to "do what I love to do."

While Seascape's menu still favors Italian fare, Jack uses the nightly specials as his opportunity to showcase dishes he likes to make — selections like the recent Pistachio Crusted Red Snapper which uses French pistachio oil — so be sure to consider all of the day's offerings before making your choice.

SLOWLY ROASTED SALMON
WITH CARAMELIZED ONION MASHED
POTATOES

SALMON

4 (6-8 oz.) salmon, cut off   White pepper
the filet, skin on, scaled   1 t. butter

Pre-heat oven to 275°. Line bottom of a sheet pan
with aluminum foil. Butter it well. Place salmon, skin
side down, on pan. Sprinkle with salt and white pepper.

Bake in the oven for 12 minutes. Skin should peel off
easily; scrape off gray, fatty substance. Replace skin.

Note: Fish may seem under-done, but it should read
120° on the thermometer. If you prefer fish more well-
done, cook 3 minutes longer.

CARAMELIZED ONION MASHED POTATOES

10 large potatoes   1½ C. milk
4 white onions, chopped   Salt, to taste
2 sticks of butter   White pepper, to taste

Peel and chop potatoes. Boil until soft. Melt half of the
butter in a sauté pan; caramelize the onions (about 4-5
minutes) to a nice dark brown color. Drain potatoes and
place in bowl. Add onions and remaining ingredients;
mash all together with potato masher or wire whisk. To
serve: Place mashed potatoes in center of plate, salmon
on top. Consider serving with steamed snap peas.

Serves four

POLENTA

½ C. coarse yellow corn meal
1 T. butter
3 T. olive oil
¼ C. chopped garlic
1½ C. heavy cream
1½ C. milk

1½ C. water
½ C. grated Parmesan cheese
3 bay leaves
¼ t. Cayenne pepper
Salt to taste

In a heavy sauce pan, cook the garlic in butter and oil until the garlic is clear.

Add the cream, milk, water, bay leaves, and pepper; bring to a boil, reduce heat. Simmer for 5 minutes.

Remove bay leaves. Bring heat back up and add corn meal slowly, stirring constantly, until slightly firm, the consistency of porridge. Add Parmesan cheese and salt. Mix to combine.

ROASTED TOMATOES

12 ripe plum tomatoes
Chopped rosemary

Salt
Olive oil

Place tomatoes on sheet pan. Add the rosemary and salt, then oil.

Cook in 350° oven for about 10 minutes, until soft.

WARM CHOCOLATE CAKE

1 stick butter, plus extra
for batter molds
2 t. flour, plus more for
dusting molds
2 large whole eggs

2 large egg yolks
¼ C. sugar
4 oz. very good
bittersweet chocolate
(ie., Valrhona, Calabut)

Pre-heat oven to 450°; coat 4 (3-3½ oz.) metal
molds with butter and lightly dust with flour.

Melt butter and chocolate over a double boiler.
Put eggs, yolks, and sugar in mixer; beat well.

Add butter and chocolate mixture, beat well.

Add flour and incorporate. Fill molds and bake at
450° for 6-8 minutes. Center of cake will look soft
but set. Invert mold on to serving plate. Cake
should be set on outside but runny on inside.

---

*Stratford's Lordship, once Great Neck, may
be named for Richard Mills, an early settler
there and large landowner. Mills was refer-
red to as his "Lordship" Mr. Mills; his
properties at the lower end became known as
his "Lordship's Meadow".*

MARNICKS
10 Washington Pkwy., Stratford
(203) 377-6288

If it seems as if *Marnicks* has always been at the end of Washington Boulevard in the Lordship, it may be because while the Quattone family has owned this landmark eatery for forty years, the original structure was built in 1890 as a bathhouse and pavilion.

When the Quattones became the owners in the 1950s, the building was a dark, short structure (the ceilings were only six feet high) with tiny windows.

Today, every seat commands a captain's view of sand and surf. The name *Marnicks* is a blending of founders Margaret's and Nick's names. The restaurant sits mere baby steps from the public beach, ready to accommodate the gustatory needs of hungry beachgoers for all three daily meals.

The atmosphere at *Marnicks* is casual and family oriented. There is also an adjacent 29 room hotel that is considered a word-of-mouth discovery by repeat vacationers who are looking for a seaside hide-a-way.

Nick Quattone suggests "coming in off the sand to sample *Marnicks*."

BAKED STUFFED CLAMS

24 quahog clams (about)
1 medium onion,
finely diced
1-2 celery stalks,
finely diced
Butter

Dash salt and pepper
¼ t. Old Bay Spice
¼ t. garlic powder
2 t. chopped parsley
3 C. dried bread crumbs
Paprika

Wash and clean the clams.

Fill a pot with about 2" of water. Bring to a boil and add the clams. Cover the pot and continue to boil until the clams pop open. Remove the clams from the pot and, after they have cooled, remove the clams from the shells. Save 12 shells (remove muscle) and reserve 1 cup of the clam broth. Chop the clams. Set aside in a bowl.

Sauté the onions and celery in the butter then add them to the chopped clams. Season with the salt, pepper, Old Bay Spice, garlic, and parsley.

Add the bread crumbs. Blend this mixture together and add enough clam broth to hold it together.

Fill the clam shells with the mixture, sprinkle with paprika and bake in a 350° oven for about 25 to 30 minutes.

Serves four

LOBSTER ROLL

2 (1-1¼ lb. each) lobsters   Toasted soft rolls
¼ lb. 100 percent butter

Put a larger pot on the stove with approximately
1" of water in the bottom. Bring the pot of water to
a boil.

Drop the two lobsters into the boiling water and
cover the pot.

Let them simmer for 5 minutes for the first pound
and then 3 minutes for each additional pound.
When done, remove and cool down.

Next, crack the shells and remove all of the leg, tail,
and claw meat. Remove the tendons. Cut into bite-
sized pieces.

Melt the butter in a pan over medium heat and drop
the lobster in.

Heat the lobster until it is hot. Remove from the
stove and spoon the lobster onto a toasted soft roll.
Make sure you get the butter onto the roll.

---

*"Our lobster rolls are our most
popular item," says Nick Quattone.*

SHRIMP CASINO

GARLIC BUTTER

½ lb. butter, softened
12 cloves of garlic,
chopped fine
Dash of black pepper

Dash of onion powder
2 T. chopped parsley
½ green pepper, minced
½ red pepper, minced

Mix all of the ingredients together until everything is
fully incorporated. Set aside.

½ red pepper, julienned
½ green pepper,
julienned
1 medium tomato, diced

½ yellow pepper,
julienned
6 strips of bacon, browned
and crumbled

Combine everything and set aside.

ASSEMBLY

24 jumbo shrimp, peeled
and deveined
Splash of white wine

Cooked pasta
Grated cheese
Chopped fresh parsley

Take Garlic Butter and place in a sauté pan. Melt
butter slowly, add shrimp and wine. When shrimp are
half cooked, turn them over and add pepper, tomato,
and bacon mixture. Toss together in a pan and turn up
the heat. Once the wine has cooked off, the shrimp are
finished. Place over cooked pasta; serve with grated
cheese and parsley.

Serves four

OUTRIGGERS
Foot of Broad St. at Brewer's Stratford Marina
(203) 377-8815

Outriggers' owner Bruce Miller has found the perfect way to blend his two loves: cooking and boating. A graduate of the Culinary Institute of America, Bruce creates what he calls "modern cuisine" with great attention to its presentation and he offers "five or six" specials daily at his restaurant which sits just feet from the water at Brewer Marina. The weekend breakfast crowd has discovered his freshly made-on-site muffins and donuts.

Outriggers' new building, with its natural gray exterior, was designed by the architect to match the other marina facilities which include a pool house. (The marina can be contacted on channel 9 for slip assignment.)

Outriggers, where ospreys have been spotted nesting in the salt marsh during blues season, gives landlubbers, especially those with children, a peek at the seafayering lifestyle — and if you time it right, you may catch one of the spectacular sunsets that comes with your meal at no extra charge.

Bruce says, "Sail away to *Outriggers* for fine dining in a relaxed atmosphere." (Now open year round.)

BAKED SCROD WITH SHERRY CRUMBS

¾ lbs. scrod filets
1 C. Japanese bread
crumbs
¼ C. sherry wine
2 T. grated cheese

1 t. fresh thyme
1 t. chopped parsley
¼ C. melted butter
Salt and pepper to taste

In a bowl, mix together all of the dry ingredients.

Add the liquid ingredients.

Place the scrod filets in a baking dish.

Top with the bread crumb mixture.

Bake at 450° for 8 to 10 minutes.

Serves two

Potatoes were viewed with suspicion for many years — making their way into the menu around 1720 — turnips, peas, beans, and pumpkins were typical fare instead.

PENNE PASTA TOSSED WITH LOBSTER, SAUSAGE, AND CHICKEN

¼ lb. grilled sausage, diced
¼ lb. grilled chicken breast, diced
¼ lb. cooked lobster meat, diced
4 T. olive oil
3 cloves garlic, crushed
¼ C. sliced portabello mushrooms
¼ C. diced sun dried tomatoes
Salt and pepper to taste
½ t. oregano
¼ C. chopped parsley
1 C. white wine
3 oz. butter
1 lb. penne pasta, cooked according to package directions

Heat the olive oil in a large sauté pan.

Add the garlic, mushrooms, and sun dried tomatoes.

Sauté until tender.

Add the sausage, chicken, lobster meat, salt and pepper, oregano, parsley, and wine.

Simmer for 2 minutes.

Add the butter and strained pasta.

Toss until the penne is evenly coated.

Serves four to six

Milford

This area was settled in 1639 as an independent colony by a congregation of English Puritans led by their minister, the Reverend Peter Prudden. Land was purchased from Ansantawae, a sachem of the Paugusset Indians, and originally named Wepawaug. It was renamed Milford in November, 1640, joined New Haven Colony in 1643, and Connecticut Colony in 1664.

Among the Regicides responsible for the trial and execution sentence of English King Charles I were William Goffe and Edward Whalley, who were sheltered here from royal authorities between 1661 and 1664.

A Connecticut group led by Robert Treat of Milford founded Newark, New Jersey, in 1666. The Reverend Samuel Andrew served as rector of Yale College from 1707 to 1719 and instructed the senior class in his home here.

Early industries included shipbuilding, oystering, seed growing, and the manufacture of carriages, boots, shoes, straw hats, and brass and bronze fabrications.

Noted ealier residents included Connecticut governors Robert Treat, Jonathan Law, and Charles Hobby Pond; colonial lawyer Jared Ingersoll; Revolutionary leaders Charles Pond and Jehiel Bryan; explorer Peter Pond; and inventors George W. Coy, Frank J. Sprague, and Simon Lake.

COSTA AZZURA
72 Broadway, Milford
(203) 878-6688

Costa Azzura's owner, Livio Faustini, may try to convince you that he discovered Milford when he swam from his native Riposte, Italy to America's shore in the 1950s. While he actually came the more traditional way, the story of how he came to be the owner of this restaurant and banquet hall directly on Long Island Sound is remarkable and worth telling.

Livio was working as a baker in Bridgeport. One Saturday night he was driving along the coast searching for a site for his dream restaurant, spotted a 'for sale' sign outside of what was then the Wildemere, had a drink, and bought the place on Monday.

The rest, as they say, is history. *Costa Azzura* is a family venture that specializes in private parties but also serves lunch and dinner. The menu primarily features southern Italian cuisine and son Benny is especially enthusiastic about their veal that is cut from the leg.

Father and son both attribute *Costa Azzura's* success to wife and mother, Nancy Faustini. They say that without her dedication and culinary talents, the place just would not exist.

85

VEAL AND SHRIMP FRANCESE

4 medallions of veal,
pounded thin
6 jumbo shrimp, peeled
and deveined
Flour for dredging
1 egg, beaten
Soybean oil for frying

2 C. chicken stock
½ C. sherry wine
½ C. butter
4 large mushrooms, sliced
Juice of half a lemon
Salt to taste

Dip the veal and shrimp in the flour.

Dip them in the beaten egg.

Heat the oil in a pan and fry the veal until it is golden on both sides.

Remove the veal from the pan and set aside.

Add the chicken stock, sherry, butter, mushrooms, lemon juice, and salt to the pan. Mix, scraping the bits on the pan bottom from cooking the veal.

Add the shrimp and return the veal to the pan.

Continue to cook until the veal and shrimp are cooked and the sauce is thick. Add a little bit of flour if sauce needs more thickening.

Serves two

VEAL MARSALA

5 medallions of veal, pounded thin
Flour for dredging
1 T. butter
Pinch fresh crushed garlic

2 large mushrooms, sliced
Fresh parsley, chopped
Salt to taste
Pepper to taste
½ - ¾ C. marsala wine

Dredge the veal in the flour.

Heat the butter in a frying pan.

Add the veal and the garlic.

Sauté quickly and flip the veal.

Add the mushroom slices, parsley, salt, pepper, and marsala wine.

Continue to cook until the veal is nicely browned with the wine sauce and the sauce has thickened.

Serves two

Costa Azzura's recipes were created by Nancy Faustini

VODKA PENNE
WITH PROSCUITTO IN CREAM SAUCE

½ C. butter
½ onion, diced
4 slices proscuitto, thinly sliced and cut into diced size pieces
2 cloves garlic, sliced
2 T. chopped fresh parsley

½ C. vodka
1 plum tomato, chopped
2 C. half and half
3 large egg yolks
½ C. grated Romano cheese
¾ lb. penne pasta, cooked

Melt the butter in a medium pan.

Add the onions, proscuitto, garlic, and parsley.

Cook for 3 to 5 minutes on medium or medium high.

Warning: Be very careful when doing the next step; the alcohol will make a flame!

Pour the vodka into the pan.

Add the plum tomatoes and cook until the pan's contents look pinkish. After the vodka has cooked off, the mixture will be nicely caramelized.

While bringing the pan to a low boil, mix together the half and half, egg yolks, and Romano cheese. Add to pan, mixing well. Serve over the penne.

Serves two

88

West Haven

West Farms (West Haven) recorded its first household in 1648. Part of the original New Haven Colony, West Farms became the separate parish of West Haven in 1719 when the Connecticut General Assembly granted a petition submitted in 1712.

West Haven and North Milford joined in 1822 to form the Town of Orange. The rural and residential sections of Orange separated in 1921 when the residential part, West Haven, became Connecticut's youngest town.

In 1961 West Haven was incorporated as a city and adopted a mayor—council form of government. By this action, one of the oldest settlements became the newest municipality in Connecticut.

JIMMIE'S OF SAVIN ROCK
5 Rock St., W. Haven
(203) 934-3212

Those of a certain age may remember when Savin Rock was a thriving amusement park with rides literally extending over Long Island Sound.

Jimmie's was there then, and after many expansions and modernizations, it's there still with its sweeping vistas of Long Island Sound right outside its windows.

The restaurant's history begins in 1925 when grandfather Sal sold his newly created 'split hot dog' from a push cart at the junction where the trolly changed directions. People would buy one of these fast cooked dogs as they waited for the trolley to turn around.

Now the third generation carries on the family tradition. *Jimmie's* is known for its fried seafood (cooked with cholesterol free oil for the last 25 years), but sautéed seafood, pasta, and non-seafood entrees are also offered.

This full-service restaurant is open seven days a week serving lunch and dinner and its banquet hall can accommodate 125 diners. After dining, consider a nice stroll down the boardwalk — mere steps from this West Haven institution.

JIMMIE'S HOUSE SALAD

½ lb. boneless chicken breast
Greens of choice: chicory, romaine, red leaf
Carrots, shredded or julienned
Cheese, any kind, julienned
Dressing: balsamic vinegar and virgin olive oil

Grill the chicken breast in the broiler for about 3 minutes on each side or until it is completely cooked.

Slice the grilled chicken into strips.

Shred the salad greens and put in a bowl.

Lay the chicken strips on top of the greens.

Add the carrots and cheese.

Whisk the balsamic vinegar and olive oil together and pour over the salad.

Serves one

Until 1875 Connecticut had two capitals — Hartford and New Haven.

SHRIMP SCAMPI

1½ lbs. shrimp (26-30/lb.), peeled and cleaned
1 lb. lightly salted butter
Garlic, minced, to taste
White pepper to taste
Salt to taste

1 bunch fresh parsley, chopped
Red pepper flakes to taste
White wine to taste
Linguini #7, cooked

Make drawn butter by simmering it in a pan and then skimming off the fat.

Cook the linguini according to package directions.

Brown the garlic very lightly in the butter.

Add the shrimp and sauté for 1½ minutes.

Add the white pepper, salt, parsley, and red pepper.

Bring the heat to a high temperature and add the white wine to taste.

Reduce the heat to low and simmer until shrimp are cooked through.

Serve the shrimp scampi over the linguini, adding a little salt and oil, if desired.

Serves four

92

FRIED CALAMARI

1 lb. squid
1 egg, beaten
Salt and white pepper, to taste
Flour for dredging
Garlic powder

Parsely, chopped
Oil for frying
Seasoned marinara sauce
Lemon wedges for garnish

Cleaning the squid:
Run the squid under cold water, filling the tubes.
Remove the beaks and the cartilage and cut the
tubes into 5/8" rings; dry well in paper towels.

Season the beaten egg with the salt and pepper.

Season the flour with the garlic powder, pepper,
and parsley; dredge the squid in the flour, shaking
off the excess. Shake well, coat well, being especially certain to coat the inside of the rings.

Heat the oil in a frying pan to 350°.

Lay the pieces in the oil and fry for about 1½
minutes. They will sink and then rise when done.
*Don't over-fill the pan because the oil's temper-
ature will be lowered and the calamari will
get soggy.*

Serve with the seasoned marinara sauce and lemon.

OYSTER RIVER TAVERN
38 Ocean Avenue, West Haven
(203) 932-0440

Oyster River Tavern was once Harry's, a neighborhood bar. In fact, Harry himself still comes by now and then. The spot was also once a stop on the Connecticut music and dance club circuit in the 1930s and the late Ella Fitzgerald was one of the headliners.

Today patrons indulge in a bacchanalian environment where smoking is permitted at every table. While the juke box plays, diners attack the plate brimming portions for which the *Oyster River Tavern* is known. Chef Pat Biancur says he strives to create innovative dishes and we "don't do anything normal. Unless someone copies it, it hasn't been seen anywhere else."

Oyster River Tavern has great views of Long Island Sound and it is located across the street from a public beach. The Oyster River is adjacent to the building.

Whether they sit in the bar or in the dining area, patrons of all ages will feel comfortable. Parents with children will find this a particularly wise choice — the *Oyster River Tavern* is not a quiet place so the smaller set will fit right in. If you're feeling blue and want to be cheered up, you'll probably enjoy *Oyster River Tavern*!

TOMATO PESTO BRUSCHETTA

4 large ripe tomatoes
½ C. pesto sauce *(Carla's brand substitutes nicely)*

2 oz. grated Pecorino Romano cheese
Butter

4 slices of Italian bread

Dice the tomatoes.

Combine and toss the diced tomatoes with the pesto and 1¾ ounces of the cheese.

Toast and lightly butter the bread.

Top the bread with the mixture.

Garnish with the remaining cheese.

Serves four

The first post road between New York and Boston passed through Providence, Stonington, and New London and extended 250 miles closely following the Old Pequot Path as far as Providence.

CHICKEN SIMEONE SANDWICH

2 fresh hard rolls	½ C. balsamic vinegar
10 oz. boneless chicken	3 oz. olive oil
breasts	2 T. honey
2 bell peppers	1 oz. sliced Muenster
3 oz. Italian dressing	cheese
2 T. red wine vinegar	Lettuce and tomato slices

Cut the peppers in half; remove the core and seeds.

Grill or broil the peppers, skin side down, until the skins are black.

Remove the peppers from the grill and cover with plastic wrap until condensation forms on top. Peel when cool enough to handle.

Marinate the chicken in the Italian dressing for 4 hours. (Add the extra red wine vinegar to the marinade.)

Marinate the grilled peppers in the balsamic vinegar, oil, and honey, for 4 hours.

Grill the chicken breasts and top with the marinated peppers. Finish with the Muenster cheese and serve on the rolls with lettuce and tomato.

Serves two

TAVERN STYLE CHICKEN SALTIMBOCCA

5 oz. boneless chicken breast, grilled and chilled	¼ C. dried sage
3 ripe tomatoes	¼ C. sherry
2 T. olive oil plus extra for roasting tomatoes	½ C. chicken stock
Salt and pepper	3 oz. salted butter
3 oz. prosciutto, thinly sliced	3 oz. grated Pecorino Romano cheese
2 T. chopped fresh parsley	1 fresh small Mozzarella ball
	Cooked pasta

Slice the grilled breast into ¼" strips.

Core the tomatoes and cut them into 6 to 8 pieces each and roast them. Roast the tomatoes by placing them on a baking sheet, season with salt and pepper and 1 to 2 oz. of olive oil; bake at 400° until the tops are brown. Remove them from the oven.

Heat a sauté pan. Add a pinch of salt, pepper, and the olive oil.

Add the proscuitto and sauté for 2 minutes.

Add the parsley and sage and sauté for another 2 minutes.

Toss in the tomatoes and sherry and let cook for 2 to 3 minutes to cook off the alcohol. *(Continued...)*

97

Add the chicken stock and bring to a boil.

Turn down to a simmer and add the butter and the Romano cheese.

Add the chicken slices.

Continue to cook until the sauce reduces and thickens.

Add the fresh mozzarella (sliced thin; always helps in melting).

When cheese is melted, lay over your favorite pasta.

Serves one

The first Connecticut man to compile an almanac (second only to the Bible in importance) was John Tully of Saybrook Point. His series continued from 1687-1702, and he "dyed as he was finishing this Almanack".

BEACH STREET WATERFRONT GRILLE
343 Beach St., West Haven
(203) 934-3554

Bobby Costanzo spent twenty years building the Original New England Food & Beverage Co. into a successful restaurant. But as the millennium approached, he decided that both he and his patrons were ready for a change.

The result is his new *Beach Street Waterfront Grille*. Bobby wanted to bring South Florida to the West Haven shoreline, and with the help of award winning architect Vladimir Shpitalnik, that's exactly what he's done. The interior is an artist's palate of vibrant rainbow hues: blues, greens, yellows, and lavenders. Cactus rest complacently along the perimeter — but the atmosphere here is definitely not subdued.

Chef Tim Collins emphasizes that some of NEF&B's menu favorites were retained, but he is now creating more contemporary cuisine. He likes to experiment with dishes, especially by using ingredients that are in season.

Be sure to take a peek into the bar if you're there at night: The evening becomes electric as hundreds of shining 'stars' light up the ceiling — creating a romantic setting, but without the mosquitoes!

CALAMARI SALAD

2½ lbs. squid, *cleaned, poached, and chilled*
¼ C. diced red onion
½ C. diced celery
¼ C. sliced black olives
½ large red roasted pepper, diced
¼ C. green pepper, diced
½ T. fresh chopped garlic

1 T. fresh lemon juice
1 T. fresh chopped parsley
1 T. fresh chopped basil
1 small hot cherry pepper, diced
Balsamic vinaigrette, enough to coat well

Combine all of the ingredients.

Let marinate at least 6 hours before serving.

Serves seven to eight

―――――――――――――――――

Beach Street Waterfront Grille's recipes were created by Chef Tim Collins

GRILLED SALMON
WITH TROPICAL FRUIT SALSA

4 fresh farm raised salmon filets (4-6 oz. each)	¼ C. garlic and herb flavored olive oil Salt and pepper to taste

TROPICAL FRUIT SALSA

½ pint strawberries, diced	1 small sweet red pepper, finely diced
2 kiwi, peeled and diced	1 T. fresh cilantro, chopped
½ C. fresh pineapple, diced	Salt and pepper to taste
½ ripe mango, diced	2 T. Malibu rum

Mix well and let stand. Re-mix.

ASSEMBLY

Coat the salmon filets with the flavored oil, and salt and pepper.

Remove the excess oil before placing the salmon on the grill.

Cook at medium heat so as not to char the fish too much.

Place the salsa over or along-side the cooked fish. Best served with rice.

Serves four

101

PECAN PIE

3 T. butter	½ C. pecans, chopped
2 t. vanilla extract	1 C. dark corn syrup
¾ C. sugar	Pinch of salt
3 large eggs	½ C. pecan halves

1 pie shell

Pre-heat oven to 450°.

Cream the butter with the vanilla extract; gradually add the sugar, creaming well.

Add the eggs, 1 at a time, beating thoroughly after each addition.

Beat in the chopped pecans, corn syrup, and salt.

Put into the un-baked pie shell.

Bake at 450° for 10 minutes.

Remove the pie from the oven and arrange the pecan halves over the top of the filling.

Lower the heat to 350°.

Return the pie to the oven and continue baking for 30 to 35 minutes.

Cool on a wire rack before serving.

CAPTAIN'S GALLEY
19 Beach Rd., West Haven
(203) 932-1811

Captain's Galley owner Paul Patrigani decided back in 1980 to make the plunge and apply his extensive restaurant experience to his own venture.

He started small with 50 seats but then expanded to 100 and now this very casual seafood house can accommodate 150 patrons.

Paul acknowledges that the place brims with diners during the hot summer months. But for those who are drawn to the shoreline during the chillier seasons, *Captain's Galley's* glowing fireplace provides a toasty, cozy, atypically quiet atmosphere for sound-gazers.

Paul, who when he can find some spare time enjoys indulging in his speed boating hobby, is proud that *Captain's Galley* is renown for the prodigious portions they serve because he says he strives to offer value portions. He also notes that his restaurant has been recognized for its prime rib, an entree choice most people don't necessarily associate with the *Galley*.

Captain's Galley is open year-round and while the seasons change, this establishment remains a constant shoreline presence.

MUSSELS WITH GARLIC SAUCE

5 lbs. mussels, cleaned
and de-bearded
½ lb. butter
3 garlic cloves, crushed

¼ C. chopped fresh
parsley
2 bottles of clam juice

In a frying pan, sauté the garlic and fresh parsley in the butter.

Add the mussels and cook until they all open.

Add the clam juice, heat, and serve hot.

Serves five

One cone of sugar, weighing ten or fifteen pounds, with honey, molasses, and maple syrup, would last a colonial family for a year.

SHRIMP SCAMPI

2 lbs. jumbo shrimp,   ½ C. sherry wine
peeled and deveined   ½ C. chopped fresh
3 T. chopped fresh garlic   parsley
¼ lb. butter   Cooked rice

In a large frying pan, brown the garlic in the butter.

Add the shrimp and sauté for about 5 minutes.

When the shrimp are ready (pink in color), add the
sherry wine and the parsley.

Simmer 2-3 minutes longer.

Serve over the rice.

Serves four

----

*Saturday night was the favorite time for the
colonists to eat baked beans.*

VEAL TIFFANY

2 lbs. veal cutlets	Asparagus tips, sliced
Flour for coating cutlets	Mushrooms, sliced
¼ C. butter	¼ C. sherry wine
2 T. finely chopped garlic	Cooked rice pilaf

Flour the cutlets.

Melt the butter in a sauté pan.

Add the garlic and sauté until the garlic is browned.

Next, brown the veal cutlets.

Add the asparagus tips and the mushrooms.

Cook for another 5 minutes.

One minute before you're finished cooking, add the sherry wine.

Serve over rice pilaf.

Serves four

CAPTAIN'S FAMOUS PRIME RIB

10 lb. rib roast   2 C. celery, cut
2 large onions, cut up   Salt and pepper

Put the rib roast in a large pan.

Cover the roast with the onions and celery.

Sprinkle the roast with salt and pepper.

Cook in the oven at 350° until the thermometer reads 120° in the center of the roast.

Serves ten

Colonial records and other sources spell the state's name many ways including: Quinniticut; Quinnihticut; Quinnehtukut; Quoneketacut; Quonahtucut; Keneticut; Conecticutt; Conecticot; Conecticotte; Conetcoit; and Connetticote

New Haven

Settlement of Quinnipiac, afterward named New Haven, began in April 25, 1638 with the arrival of a large group from London by way of Boston, under the leadership of merchant Theophilus Eaton and the Reverend John Davenport. Later that year, the present downtown area was laid out and mapped in nine squares with a central common, now called the New Haven Green. This is the first example of a planned community in the United States. The town was invaded by the British in 1779 during the Revolutionary War, but escaped serious damage, despite extensive plundering.

The City of New Haven was incorporated in 1784 and its first mayor was Roger Sherman, the only person who signed all four of the Nation's founding documents: the Articles of Association, the Declaration of Independence, the Articles of Confederation, and the Constitution of the United States.

New Haven Harbor, the largest port on Long Island Sound, was the scene of an active fishing and sailing trade in the 19th century.

New Haven in 1840 was the setting for the Amistad trial, in which 52 black slaves, who had mutinied aboard a Spanish slave ship of that name after being kidnapped in Africa in defiance of law, were cleared of all civil charges brought against them.

The city later became noted for manufacturing. New Haven is the site of a number of schools of higher learning, including Yale University, founded in 1701, South Central Community, Southern Connecticut State, and Albertus Magnus colleges, and Berkeley Divinity School. The homes and many institutional buildings of New Haven reflect the work of noted architects from the 18th century to the present. Since the 1950's, New Haven has received national acclaim for its efforts to renew and preserve the downtown and distinctive neighborhoods.

RUSTY SCUPPER
501 Long Wharf Dr., New Haven
(203) 777-5711

The *Rusty Scupper* has re-created itself for the next century. Established in 1985 in the Long Wharf section of New Haven, the interior has been completely renovated to produce an entirely new dining environment with an entirely new look.

But the two characteristics for which the *Rusty Scupper* was renown have been retained and enhanced: the cuisine and the water views.

Chef Michael Copeland says "the menu features a balance of the best seafood, shellfish, Angus beef and New England dishes blessed with the freshest ingredients served in a contemporary manner". The menu changes seasonally with salmon and tuna featured year-round.

Every seat at the *Rusty Scupper* has a dramatic view of New Haven Harbor and Long Wharf, a view difficult to appreciate when navigating I-95.

And speaking of Long Wharf, if an evening at the theater is on your agenda, the *Rusty Scupper* has just what you need: a pre-theater menu that will allow you to get to the show before the curtain rises.

110

MUSSELS WITH TOMATO FENNEL BROTH, BRAISED LEEKS AND PURPLE BASIL

TOMATO FENNEL BROTH

1 T. oil
1 C. onions, rough cut ½"
2 C. fennel, rough cut ½"
(use some stems and scrap
pieces)
2 C. tomatoes, cut 2"

1 C. white wine
1 bay leaf
2 C. water
1 t. salt
¼ t. pepper
¼ C. pernod

In a sauce pot, heat the oil and sweat the onions and fennel. Add tomatoes, wine and bay leaf; reduce by half.

Add the water, salt, and pepper; simmer for 30 minutes. Add the pernod. Puree, strain through a sieve, cool and reserve.

ASSEMBLY

18 P. E. I. mussels,
cleaned
1 t. oil
½ t. minced garlic (⅛")
1 t. minced shallots (⅛")
¼ C. leeks, white only,
julienned ⅛" x 2"
½ C. tomato fennel broth

1 t. purple basil, ⅛"
chiffonade
½ t. salt
¼ t. pepper
1 T. tomato concasse
(peeled, seeded and
diced ¼")

Heat a sauté pan. When it is hot, add the oil, garlic, shallots, and leeks. *(Continued...)*

111

Cook until they are soft, but do not brown.

Add the mussels and tomato fennel broth.

Cover the pan; steam until the mussels open.

Add the basil, salt, pepper, and tomato concasse.

Arrange in hot 12" pasta bowl and top with a little more basil.

Consider serving with taglatelle pasta which is slightly wider than fettucini.

Serves one

Rusty Scupper's recipes were created by Chef Michael Copeland

112

MONK FISH "OSSO BUCCO" WITH SAFFRON ORZO SALAD AND TOMATO FENNEL RELISH

SAFFRON ORZO SALAD

1 lb. orzo pasta
½ t. saffron
1 gallon water
Salt
¾ C. zucchini, seeds removed, diced ¼"
1 C. blanched asparagus, cut ¼"
½ C. red pepper, diced ¼"

½ C. scallions, diced ¼"
¼ C. red onions, ⅛" dice
¼ C. fresh parsley, washed and dried, chopped ⅛"
½ C. balsamic vinaigrette
1 t. salt
¼ t. black pepper
¼ C. basil, chopped ¼"

Cook orzo in boiling saffron water (1 gallon water, saffron, and enough salt so it almost tastes like the ocean). Cool and add to the other ingredients. Toss.

Yields seven cups

SCALLION OIL

4 C. oil
¼ lb. scallions

¼ T. salt
¼ t. black pepper

Puree all in a blender until the scallions are very fine. Refrigerate for 24 hours. Strain through a fine sieve, reserve green oil and put in a squirt bottle to use as needed.

Yields one quart   *(Continued...)*

TOMATO FENNEL RELISH

1 C. fennel, ¼" dice
1 C. tomato concasse
(peeled, seeded, diced ¼")
¼ C. basil chiffonade ¼"
2 T. balsamic vinegar

¼ C. extra virgin olive oil
½ t. salt
¼ t. cracked black
pepper

Mix all together; let sit at least 8 hours.

Yields 1 pint

FINAL ASSEMBLY

2 (4 oz. each) pieces of
monkfish, with bone
Flour for dredging
Oil
1 t. salt
¼ t. pepper
3 oz. Tomato Fennel
Relish*

¾ C. Saffron Orzo Salad*
1 T. Balsamic Glaze**
1 t. chopped chives, ¼"
2 T. Scallion oil
Room temperature
(Optional) Heat some
balsamic vinegar in a pan
until a syrup is formed.

Season the monkfish with salt and pepper, dredge
in flour and shake off all the loose flour.

In a hot sauté pan with oil, sear the monkfish.

Finish in the oven until it is golden brown.

(Continued...)

114

Place the Orzo Salad in the center of a plate.

Arrange the Osso Bucco on top of the orzo, fanned out half on salad, half off toward 6 o'clock position.

Top with Fennel Relish.

Finish with balsamic drizzle, chives, and Scallion Oil around the salad.

Serves one

When Connecticut had two capitals, Hartford and New Haven, the May Assembly met in Hartford and the October Assembly met in New Haven.

115

BERRY BERRY SHORTCAKE

1 dessert biscuit, cut in half
1 C. Berries in Glaze
¾ C. sweetened whipped cream*

*Whip together 1 C. of heavy cream with 1 T. of confectioner's sugar and Amaretto or other appropriate flavor

BERRIES IN GLAZE

½ C. strawberries, sliced
8 whole raspberries
8 blueberries
8 blackberries
¼ C. Strawberry Glaze*

* Heat equal parts of strawberry jam and water over low heat until the mixture is syrupy.

Gently mix the berries and Strawberry Glaze together. Warm the biscuit in the microwave then place the bottom half of the warmed biscuit on a dessert plate. Place ¼ C. of the whipped cream on the biscuit. Top the whipped cream with half of the Berries in Glaze, making sure the blueberries and raspberries are showing.

On top of the berries, place ¼ C. of the whipped cream. Top with the remaining Berries in Glaze, again making sure the blueberries and raspberries are showing. On top of the berries, place the top half of the biscuit, and finish with the rest of the whipped cream.

Serves one

116

CHART HOUSE
100 South Water St., New Haven
(203) 787-3466

There are four *Chart House* restaurants in Connecticut, with the ones in Greenwich and New Haven located on the coast, both just short detours from Interstate 95.

The New Haven *Chart House* is a 'test restaurant': all of the newest food items, service enhancement ideas, lounge promotions, and drink specials are experienced by patrons there first. The *Chart House* considers itself an interactive restaurant — one night diners were treated to a free sample of a new drink, a saffron martini.

Excellent food served with impeccable service is stressed at this harbor-side establishment where every seat in its open and spacious two story modern space has a water view. The goal here is to make guests feel pampered, as if they're on a little vacation a lá Club Med.

The *Chart House* recognizes that cigar smoking has become more popular and wide-spread, so they've made the patio cigar-friendly. Also, after 10 p.m., cigar smoking is permitted in the lounge — where "business-people can smoke cigars, sip a cognac, and close that important deal."

BLEU CHEESE DRESSING

¾ C. sour cream
½ t. dry mustard
½ t. black pepper
½ t. salt
⅓ t. garlic powder

1 t. Worcestershire sauce
1⅓ C. mayonnaise
4 oz. imported Danish
bleu cheese, crumbled

Combine the sour cream, dry mustard, black pepper, salt, garlic powder, and Worcestershire sauce.

Blend for 2 minutes at low speed.

Add the mayonnaise and blend for 30 seconds at low speed, then increase the speed to medium and blend for an additional 2 minutes.

Slowly add the bleu cheese and blend at low speed no longer than 4 minutes.

Refrigerate for 24 hours before serving.

Yields 2½ Cups

The site now known as New Haven was originally called Quinnipiac or Quillipiac.

STEAMED SHELLFISH
WITH TOAST POINTS

SHELLFISH BROTH

½ C. water   1 C. clam juice
½ C. white wine   2 T. lemon juice
2 T. chopped fresh thyme   ¾ t. black pepper
1 T. minced fresh garlic   ½ t. kosher salt

Combine all ingredients. Mix well. Refrigerate in a
sealed container until needed. *Use within 2 days.*

Yields 1 pint

TOAST POINTS

½ lb. butter   ¼ t. kosher salt
¼ C. olive oil   ½ C. Parmesan cheese,
1 T. roasted garlic puree   shaved
¼ t. black pepper   1 French baguette, sliced
½ T. chopped Italian   ½" x 3½" thick
parsley

In a sauce pan, combine and melt butter and olive oil
over medium heat. Add the remaining ingredients,
except the bread, and blend well. Lay out the bread
slices on a sheet pan and brush each piece with about
1 T. of the melted butter/olive oil mixture. Bake in a
pre-heated 350° oven for 8 to 10 minutes or until
golden brown and slightly crispy. *(Continued...)*

Serves six

STEAMED SHELLFISH WITH TOAST POINTS
(...continued)

STEAMED SHELLFISH AND ASSEMBLY

1 lb. mussels, de-bearded
and rinsed *or* clams,
cleaned and rinsed
½ C. shellfish broth

1 t. chopped parsley
Toast points (2 for each
serving)

Place the shellfish in a sauté pan with the broth.

Place the pan over medium high heat, cover and
cook the shellfish about 3 minutes.

Remove the pan from the heat and toss to coat the
shellfish with the heated broth. Return the pan to the
stove and continue cooking for another 3 minutes.

Remove the pan from the heat and toss again. This
time the shells should have opened.

Transfer the shellfish and broth to a warm pasta
bowl and sprinkle with the chopped parsley.

Place 2 toast points, tip facing out, on opposite sides
of the bowl and serve immediately.

Serves one

MUD PIE

4½ oz. chocolate wafers
¼ C. butter, melted
1 gal. coffee ice cream, soft
1½ C. fudge sauce*
Diced almonds
Whipped cream

It helps to put the fudge sauce in the freezer for a while to make spreading easier

Crush the wafers and add the butter.

Mix well.

Press into a 9" pie plate.

Cover with soft coffee ice cream.

Top with cold fudge sauce.

Store the Mud Pie in the freezer for approximately 10 hours before serving.

When serving, slice the Mud Pie into 8 portions and serve on chilled dessert plates.

Top with whipped cream and diced almonds.

Serves eight

AMARANTE'S
62 Cove St., New Haven
(203) 467-2531

Andy Amarante is the patriarch of this multi-facetted establishment on New Haven Harbor that bears his name. His six children have all followed him into the business.

The owner brings a life-time of culinary expertise to this special destination. He took over the space, which was then an inn, in 1966 and he has been renovating and modernizing and expanding it ever since.

The restaurant is primarily set aside for private parties, but for the last decade-plus, during mid-week, *Amarante's* turns its ballroom into a family-oriented dinner theatre complete with a buffet and separate dessert table.

The 'Clam Shed', located near the patio, offers a full-menu that can be enjoyed outside at water's edge. Diners can scan the New Haven skyline across the Sound. On a clear day, Andy says you can see Woodmont.

Andy Amarante is a gregarious host who says, "I don't care if people come and spend a lot of money or not. I'd like them to enjoy the sweeping views and ambience. Just come to *Amarante's* and enjoy."

MUSHROOM POTATO CAKES

3 potatoes, peeled and
diced
2 T. butter
½ lb. mushrooms, sliced
thin

1 shallot, minced
1 egg, lightly beaten
Salt and pepper, to taste
½ C. vegetable oil

Cook the potatoes until tender, drain, and place in a
mixing bowl.

Heat butter over medium heat, add the mushrooms
and shallot and cook over high heat until the
mushrooms are cooked and any moisture they
release has cooked away.

Add the mushrooms and shallots to the potatoes.

Add the egg, salt, and pepper and combine.

Cool, shape it into large or small cakes.

Heat the oil over high heat.

Add the potato cakes and cook for about
2 to 3 minutes per side or until they are golden
brown.

Drain on paper towels and serve hot.

ONE DISH CHICKEN

Aluminum foil*
Chicken pieces
Green pepper, sliced
Mushrooms, quartered
Small onion, sliced
Cherry tomatoes

Small potatoes, cut in half
or quartered
Worcestershire sauce
Salt and pepper
Butter

*The quantities of each ingredient depends upon the
number of servings being prepared*

Cut off large pieces of aluminum foil for each
dinner guest.

Fold foil in half.

Place chicken piece, pepper, mushroom, onion,
tomato, and potato on the foil.

Sprinkle with Worcestershire sauce, salt and pepper,
and a little butter.

Fold foil over.

Bake in 450° oven for about 45 minutes.

Turn the package every 20 minutes.

CHOCOLATE FRUIT

1 lb. semi-sweet chocolate   Strawberries, pineapple,
1 T. vegetable shortening   or any desired peeled fruit

Chop the chocolate into small pieces.

In a double boiler, combine the chocolate and the shortening.

Heat the pot until the chocolate melts and the mixture is smooth.

Remove the pot from the heat, but keep the chocolate mixture over the hot water.

Dip each strawberry or piece of pineapple or desired fruit into the mixture to coat.

Place each dipped piece of fruit on a rack or a piece of waxed paper.

The coating will set in about 10 to 15 minutes.

*Amarante's recipes were created
by Chef Russell Dallaire*

East Haven

This area, purchased by the Reverend John Davenport and Theophilus Eaton in 1638, was later known as East Farms. It was obtained from Indian sachems Momaugin and Mantowese.

In 1639 Thomas Gregson, the first landowner, purchased Solitary Cove, later called Morris Cove. The first Connecticut ironworks was located in 1655 by Lake Saltonstall, formerly named Lonotononket, then Furnace Pond. East Farms became known as Iron Works Village, the third iron industry in the New England colonies.

Jacob Heminway, the original Yale student, served as the first pastor (1704-1757) of the Congregational Church. In 1774 the Old Stone Church was erected; its first minister was Nicholas Street.

This area was invaded in 1779 by British General William Tryon. During the Revolutionary War, Lafayette encamped on the Green, revisiting it in 1824.

In 1881 Fair Haven, Granniss Corners, and Morris Cove were ceded to New Haven.

The Roosevelt Turkey Oak, a gift from President Theodore Roosevelt, was planted on the Green in 1908.

The initial town meeting (1785) named Issac Chidsey First Selectman. The town became a city during the 1970's under Mayor Francis W. Messina.

BEACHHEAD
3 Cosey Beach Ave., East Haven
(203) 469-5450

The *Beachhead Restaurant* is a 56 year old East Haven landmark and historic building that was first named and opened by Josephine Orifice in 1942. Josie established many traditions over the years, like her special way of frying fish.

Barbara Bucci and Cynthia Fucci understand the importance of respecting tradition and they continue to offer many of Josie's signature creations like zuppa de pesce and scampi. But they have also brought their own unique styles and interpretations to *Beachhead*, beginning with the addition of the Fbucci lounge. There is also a new upper deck and upstairs private party room now holds court where the Orifice family lived in the 1940s. Of course, the views of Long Island Sound only get better.

It is not unusual for people to return again and again to *Beachhead*. Barbara, who can be recognized by her omnipresent trademark hat, recalls a couple who had their first date there, became engaged there, and recently returned to *Beachhead* to celebrate their 37th wedding anniversary.

Beachhead will always be a restaurant where many memories begin and continue.

ORIGINAL BEACHHEAD SCROD

4 (6 oz.) scrod filets
12 oz. can plum tomatoes
1 onion, sliced
1 t. minced fresh garlic

2 sprigs fresh basil
¼ C. extra virgin olive oil
Salt and pepper to taste

TOPPING

¼ C. bread crumbs
½ t. minced fresh garlic

3 bay leaves, finely
crushed

Combine all of the topping ingredients. Set aside.

ASSEMBLY

Place the scrod in an oven proof casserole dish.

Cover the scrod with the plum tomatoes, sliced onion, minced garlic, and fresh basil.

Drizzle with the olive oil and salt and pepper.

Bake at 400° for 15 minutes.

Cover with the bread crumb topping and bake for an additional 5 minutes or until golden brown.

Serve with mashed potatoes and fresh vegetables.

Serves four

MUSSELS ALLA FBUCCI

16 mussels, cleaned and
de-bearded
2 T. olive oil
2 cloves garlic, chopped
½ C. clam juice
Pinch of fresh basil

Pinch of fresh parsley
1 C. crushed Italian
tomatoes
Salt and pepper to taste
Toasted Italian bread
points

Sauté the garlic in the oil.

Add the mussels, clam juice, basil, parsley, tomatoes, and salt and pepper.

Simmer for 5 minutes or until the mussels open.

Serve with the toasted Italian bread points.

Serves four

The Dutch called today's New Haven area Rodenberg which means Red Hill, doubtless from the predominately red color of East and West Rocks visible to mariners approaching the harbor.

130

KEY LIME PIE

5 large egg yolks
1¼ can sweented
condensed milk
½ C. lime juice

9" Graham cracker crust
Garnish: fresh lime slices
Whipped cream

Pre-heat oven to 350°.

Beat the egg yolks, condensed milk, and lime juice together.

Pour into the graham cracker crust.

Bake in a 350° oven for 15 to 20 minutes.

Garnish each serving with whipped cream and a slice of fresh lime.

New Haven was laid out in nine equal squares with streets crossing each other at right angles and a large center space for a market.

Branford

In 1638 the New Haven Colony traded "eleven coats of trucking cloth and one coat of English cloth made in the English fashion" to the Mattabesec Indians for land known as Totokett (Tidal River). The first permanent settlement was established in 1644 when people from Wethersfield came to Totokett, later renamed Branford after the town of Brentford in Middlesex County, England.

The Sound provided many of the settlers with a livelihood of shipbuilding and coastwise trade. Industry began in 1655 when the first iron furnace in Connecticut was set up and operated at Lake Saltonstall. Yale College was founded in 1701 when ten ministers met and made a contribution of books. In 1852 upon completion of the railroad, industrialization flourished. Two leading manufacturing firms were founded during this era: the Malleable Iron Fittings Company in 1854, and the Branford Lock Works in 1862. The 20th century has brought some changes to Branford, but much of its historical heritage remains in the form of old buildings and well-preserved villages.

SAM'S DOCKSIDE

Block Island Rd., Branford
(203) 481-4360

Sam's Dockside is named after owner Nick Colavolpe's daughter Samantha. Launched as a snack bar in 1992, the response was so tremendous that Nick expanded the business into a full-service sit-down restaurant that rests amid the boats at Bruce & Johnson's Marina.

Ten Colavolpe family members, including wife Lisa, keep the restaurant running smoothly, no small feat during the hectic summer season when it's not unusual to see patrons returning two and three times a week. (*Sam's Dockside* closes from October until April.)

Nick started his working life in the restaurant business, and although he took a short detour as a high school teacher he was lured back to his first love: food and the food business.

Take the time to look at the finely detailed antique ship model that is displayed in the front window. If your dinner conversation lags, read the poem that rests near the ship model: it wittily compares and contrasts women and ships; its message will surely provide you with something to chew on along with your meal in this totally smoke-free restaurant.

133

GARLIC CALAMARI

1 lb. calamari, cleaned	4 T. diced red peppers
4 oz. butter or margarine	Black pepper to taste
4 T. diced onion	¼ C. fresh lemon juice
4 garlic cloves, chopped	Chopped fresh parsley

1 lb. warm cooked rice

Slice the calamari into ½" rounds.

Sauté the onions in butter over medium heat.

Add calamari, garlic, red peppers, and black pepper.

Cook on medium heat for 5 to 9 minutes or until the calamari is firm.

Add lemon juice and chopped parsley.

Serve over warm rice.

Serves three to four

New Haven was settled by an aristocracy who built large and stately homes. Theophilus Eaton's house was built in the shape of the letter E, and Rev. John Davenport's house in the form of a cross.

BALSAMIC AND BASIL TUNA

1 lb. fresh tuna, cubed	Half a lemon
2 T. butter or oil	Coarse ground black
½ oz. balsamic vinegar	pepper, to taste

Heat the butter or oil in a pan.

Sear the tuna over high heat until the tuna is 80% cooked.

Turn the tuna over a high heat for 1 minute.

Splash with the balsamic vinegar, the juice of the half lemon, and the black pepper.

Toss for 1 minute and serve hot.

Serves three to four

Wampum currency was black and white beads about a quarter of an inch long, the black being made of mussel shells and worth twice the value of the white which came from the inside of the conch shell.

HONEY LEMON SALMON

1 lb. salmon, cubed   1 T. honey
2 T. butter or margarine   Black pepper, to taste
2 T. golden raisins   Cooked rice
¼ C. fresh lemon juice

Sauté everything, except the rice, together over low to medium heat for 4 to 5 minutes.

Be careful not to burn the honey.

Serve over hot rice.

Serves two to three

West Rock was once named "Providence Hill". Edward Whalley and William Goffe hid from King Charles I's officers in the cave there, it is said, for six months with the complicity of the area people.

Guilford

This town, the seventh oldest in Connecticut, was founded in 1639 by an oppressed but optimistic band of English Puritans. Henry Whitfield, a minister in Ockley, near London, was the moving spirit behind their emigration. About 40 of his friends and sympathizers formed a joint stock company to sail across the Atlantic. They were mostly young and energetic men, farmers, well-educated, and all of them persons of high standing in their community. In a deed of sale dated September 29, 1639, the Whitfield Company purchased the lands between Stony Creek and East River from the Squaw Shaumpishuh, Sachem of the local Menunkatuck Indian Tribe. Whitfield's stone house at first served as a fortress and meeting place. Guilford Green was inspired by the typical 17th century English common. In the fall of 1641 the settlers purchased from the Indians land beyond East River that included most of what became East Guilford. East Guilford, now Madison, was set off as a distinct church society in 1703, North Guilford in 1720, and North Bristol (North Madison) in 1753. Two good harbors and two tidal rivers assured success to Guilford in Connecticut—New York coast-wise shipping and West India trade during the 18th century.

In the American Revolution, British troops landed several times and burned two houses. The famous Sachem's Head Hotel (1832-1865) and Guilford Point House (1797-1897) made this town the center of society for many years.

John Beattie's granite quarries at Leet's Island employed as many as 300 workmen and supplied stone for the pedestal of the Statue of Liberty in New York Harbor. Famous sons of Guilford include William Leete, an early Governor of Connecticut; Firtz-Greene Halleck, one of the noted Knickerbocker Poets; and Abraham Baldwin, a signer of the United States Constitution and Senator from Georgia.

STEAMERS BAR & GRILL
505 Whitfield St., Guilford
(203) 458-1757

Steamers is a lively place where owners Jennifer and Paul Olson pay attention to the little things as they create novel ways to insure that patrons have a good time.

Located at the end of Whitfield Street just before the public boat launch, *Steamers* specializes in traditional New England seafood and steaks.

For children, there are crayons and coloring books to use while waiting to be served. Beer aficionados will find no fewer than eighteen varieties of beer on tap. And young and old can pass the time playing one of the many board games that are available at the bar. Smokers and non-smokers each have their own dining rooms — both with water views.

Details are important to Jennifer and she suggests diners sign the guestbook so she can let patrons know about coming special events.

But lest anyone think *Steamers* has forgotten it's a restaurant, the same attention to detail takes place in the kitchen: the menu is changed twice a year so the chef can be creative using the best seasonal ingredients.

STEAMERS STEEPED IN A GARLIC CHARDONNAY BROTH

1½ lbs. of steamers; soak in water to remove sand
1 qt. of water
½ C. white wine
1 C. clam juice
1 T. chopped garlic
¼ small onion, diced
2 celery stalks, chopped
Pinch of crushed red pepper
½ stick butter or margarine
1 lemon, sliced into wedges

Put the quart of water into a pot and add wine, clam juice, garlic, diced onions, celery, and red pepper (everything except steamers, butter and lemon).

Bring the pot to a boil.

Add the steamers and cook until the steamers begin to open; about 3 to 5 minutes.

Melt the butter in a pan.

Serve the steamers in a bowl with the broth and place a small cup of broth on the side so diners can rinse the steamers before dipping them in butter.

Garnish with the lemon wedges.

Serves two

PARCHMENT BAKED ATLANTIC SALMON

4-6 oz. filet of salmon,
de-boned
4 artichoke hearts,
quartered
1 medium tomato, large
dice
1 T. lemon juice

1 T. white wine
Pinch of parsley
Pinch of basil
Pinch of dill
1 piece of parchment
paper or aluminum foil

Pre-heat the oven to 425°.

Fold the parchment paper in half so it is
approximately 12" x 12".

Place everything, including the salmon, inside the fold.

Close all open ends by folding tightly.

Bake at 425° for 15 to 20 minutes.

To serve, place the packet on a plate.

Do NOT unroll the parchment paper!

Make a slit in the packet so the steam can escape.

Serves one

141

GRILLED BRIE WITH ROASTED GARLIC DRIZZLED WITH PESTO

½ loaf of Italian bread   2 T. oil
8 cloves of garlic, peeled   ¼ C. pesto
Individual wheel of Brie   2 strawberries

Slice the bread into strips, then bake at 350° until golden brown.

Prepare the garlic cloves:
Place the garlic cloves on an oiled cookie sheet. Bake in the oven at 350° until they are brown. Set them aside. Leave oven on for later step.

Prepare the Brie *(optional)*:
Grill the outside of the Brie for 15 seconds on each side to add char marks to the rind. Grilling the Brie is optional because it will not change the flavor if this step is omitted. It is used as part of a garnish.

Bake the Brie in the pre-heated 350° oven for 2 to 3 minutes or until it is soft. Place the Brie in the center of a plate and surround it with the baked bread strips.

Cover a third of the Brie with the pesto and place the garlic cloves on top of the pesto. Garnish with two whole strawberries.

Serves four

142

STONE HOUSE
506 Whitfield St., Guilford
(203) 458-2526

The *Stone House* is located in a landmark rough-hewn granite building that was built in 1949 as a restaurant by Frank and Joe Dolan. The driveway is 'paved' with shells and children will especially enjoy crunching their way to the entrance. Owners Richard Rosamilia and Ken Milio, two experienced restaurateurs, have completely remodeled this restaurant, located across from the town dock —the water is a mere 50 feet across the street. Its new official name is *Stone House Seaside Restaurant*.

There are four dining areas, each decorated differently and with a different name, like the Beckwith Room and the Wine Room. The main dining room can seat 200.

Chef Vito Bonanno says that while *Stone House* only serves lunch on Saturdays at present, they do offer Sunday brunch. The menu features off-the-boat traditional seafood; grilled steak and fish; and king crab and lobster — with lighter fare like salads and burgers also offered.

There is no question *Stone House* is family oriented — Richard's young daughter Angela had a hand in creating the children's menu, creating the artwork on a computer using nautical clip art.

SCALLOPS WITH BASIL PESTO

½ lb. bay scallops
1 T. olive oil
1 garlic clove, chopped
fine
¼ C. fish stock

3 oz. white wine
½ C. pre-made Bechamel
sauce
3 oz. fresh basil pesto
Cooked fettucini for one

Heat the olive oil.

Sauté the garlic, add the fish stock, wine, Bechamel sauce, and pesto.

Bring to a simmer.

Add the scallops and cook for 2 minutes.

Toss with cooked fettucini.

Serves one

*Stone House recipes were created by
Chef Vito Bonanno and Richard Rosamilia*

144

SAUTÉED SPINACH WITH SAUSAGE

1 T. olive oil
8 oz. fresh spinach,
picked over
1 garlic clove, sliced

2 oz. chorizo sausage,
sliced ¼" thick
Splash of white wine

Heat the oil.

Slightly brown the garlic, add the chorizo.

Sauté for about 1 minute.

Add the spinach and the splash of wine.

Cook until the spinach is wilted.

Serves one

The Henry Whitfield House in Guilford is the oldest house in Connecticut and the oldest stone house in New England.

PORTUGUESE FISHERMAN'S STEW

2 oz. butter
1 garlic clove, chopped
fine
½ C. fish stock
1 small pinch of saffron
¼ C. white wine
2 oz. chorizo sausage,
sliced ¼"

¼ C. marinara sauce
7 oz. mussels, in shell
4 shrimp, shells off
3 oz. scrod, cut
¼ lb. bay scallops
¼ C. chopped clams
Cooked linguini

Heat the butter and add the garlic.

Sauté 1 minute.

Add the fish stock, saffron, wine, chorizo sausage, and the marinara sauce.

Bring to a simmer; add the mussels, shrimp, and scrod.

Sauté 1 minute.

Add scallops, then clams.

Simmer, covered, for 2 to 3 minutes.

Let rest covered for about 2 minutes before serving.

Serve over linguini.

Serves one

Madison

This area, formerly part of Guilford and known as East Guilford, was first settled about 1650 on land bought from the Nehantic and Mohegan Indians in 1641.

With population increasing, settlers here sought separate parishes and the Society of East Guilford was incorporated in 1707, the Society in North Madison, called North Bristol, in 1753.

The town of Madison, named for President James Madison, was incorporated in 1826.

This was once a center for fishing, shipping, shipbuilding, farming, and crayon manufacturing.

Famous people born here included Thomas Chittenden, first Governor of Vermont; philanthropist Daniel Hand; artist Gilbert Munger; and chief sponsor of the Civil War ironclad warship *Monitor*, Cornelius Scranton Bushnell.

THE WHARF
The Madison Beach Hotel, 94 West Wharf Rd., Madison
(203) 245-0005

The Wharf at the Madison Beach Hotel, a resort and restaurant, is now run by the third generation of the Cooney-Bagdasarian family, a family with deep Madison roots.

In the 1900s, whaling ships were built here; the men ate in a cafeteria downstairs. Eventually the ship building business's owners opened up public rooms.

Today the *Wharf* has two separate dining rooms, both with the same menu. The informal upstairs Crow's Nest doubles as the bar and entertainment center where live bands perform an eclectic variety of danceable music from classic rhythm and blues to jazz and original rock and roll. The main floor dining room is casually formal and smoking is banned.

In 1984, the hotel was remodeled. Beth Cooney describes the hotel as quaint, with modern amenities and decorated with period prints and lots of original furniture. Each of the 35 rooms is ocean front with views of Tuxis and Faulkners Islands, and Long Island.

Beth says "Madison's shore is well kept little secret, tucked away, but close to town."

148

TUNA BURGER

1 lb. fresh tuna, finely chopped
1 shallot, peeled and minced
3 oz. capers, drained and chopped
¼ C. chives, minced
1 T. olive oil

1 T. Dijon mustard
1 t. sherry vinegar
1 t. Worcesterhire sauce
Tabasco pepper sauce, a few drops
⅓ C. parsley, chopped
Salt and pepper to taste

Mix all of the ingredients into a bowl; roughly puree about one quarter of the mixture at a time, then form the mixture into a burger.

Repeat this process 4 times; 1 pound of tuna will yield 4 burgers.

Grill the tuna burgers.

Spicy or Cajun tartar sauce is a nice accompaniment to the tuna burgers.

Serves four

The "Connecticut Gazette" of New Haven was the colony's first newspaper in 1755. It was a two-column weekly.

CRAB CAKES

1 lb. lump blue crab, pick out cartilage
½ large red pepper, diced
½ large green pepper, diced
¼ C. parsley, chopped
½ C. mayonnaise

¼ C. Dijon mustard
1 T. Cajun seasoning
Salt and pepper to taste
1½ C. bread crumbs
Clarified butter for sautéing

Reserve some of the bread crumbs.

Mix together the crab, red and green peppers, parsley, mayonnaise, mustard, seasoning, and salt and pepper.

Slowly mix in the bread crumbs using more or less depending on the moistness of the mixture. The mixture needs to be moist enough to shape into patties.

Shape the crab mixture into 4 to 6 large cakes or 8 to 12 smaller cakes for an appetizer. Roll the patties in the reserved bread crumbs.

Sauté the patties in clarified butter until they are golden brown.

Drain the patties on paper towels before serving.

Yields four to six large cakes

PUMPKIN SPICE MOUSSE

6 T. water	½ t. ground ginger
1 envelope gelatin	¼ t. ground cloves
4 egg yolks	2 T. dark rum
1 C. sugar	1 T. vanilla
16 oz. solid pack pumpkin	2 C. whipping cream
1 t. ground cinnamon	

Pour 4 T. of the water into a small bowl and sprinkle the gelatin over the top; let stand for 10 minutes.

Fill the bottom of a double boiler with water and whisk the egg yolks with the sugar and the remaining water in the top bowl over *medium heat.*

Continue to whisk until the mixture reaches 170°.

Remove from the heat and add the gelatin.

Continue mixing with an electric mixer until the mixture cools. Add pumpkin, spices, rum, and vanilla.

Refrigerate for a minimum of 30 minutes.

Whip the cream to soft-firm peaks. Fold into the pumpkin mix. Refrigerate overnight (4 hours minimum).

Serves six

Clinton

Settled in 1663 and then known as Homonoscitt Plantation, this shoreline and rural community soon thereafter was given the name Kenilworth and later Killingworth. In 1735 the First and Second Ecclesiastical Societies were established, being the southern and northern portions of the Town respectively. In May 1838, the southern portion was incorporated as a separate town with the name of Clinton after DeWitt Clinton, Governor of New York. Early classes of the Collegiate School, later Yale University, were held here.

Citizens prominent in Clinton history include Abraham Pierson, a founder and first rector of the Collegiate School; Jared Eliot, church pastor and noted doctor, friend of Benjamin Franklin; Benjamin Gale, pupil of Eliot, gifted physician and agriculturist; Charles Morgan, benefactor of public schools; and Horatio G. Wright, Civil War general, chief of army engineers

AQUA RESTAURANT
34 Riverside Dr., Clinton
(860) 664-3788

Nestled dockside at the Cedar Island Marina, *Aqua Restaurant* greets patrons with its inviting bright aqua blue exterior. Inside, a clear view of Cedar Island and water activities are a glance away.

Owner and Chef Rob Johnson takes pride in serving what he calls 'simple food' — food without pretense that is meant to be savored for its quality and taste.

Aqua has a few different personalities: the large dining area, which looks out upon the water, is smoke-free, but the bar has tables for dining and smoking. There is a 'soft seating area' with comfy living-room furniture where people can either sit while waiting for a table or just converse after a day on the water.

The fieldstone fireplace in the bar warms the air on crisp non-summer nights. Two 7 foot tall woodcarved bears watch over the room and are worth admiring even if the bar isn't your destination.

Rob invites travelers who are journeying by land or by sea to come to *Aqua* year-round to sample his cuisine.

SHRIMP ARREGANATA

8 medium shrimp, peeled
and cleaned
2 T. extra-virgin olive oil
2 large cloves of garlic,
chopped fine

½ C. bread crumbs
Salt and pepper to taste
Melted butter or olive oil
Lemon wedges

Lightly brown the garlic in the olive oil.

Let cool 5 minutes.

Stir in bread crumbs and salt and pepper.

Brush the shrimp with melted butter or olive oil.

Lay the shrimp in an oven-proof dish.

Sprinkle the bread crumb mixture on the shrimp.
Do not smother the shrimp.

Place in a 400° oven and cook until the bread
crumb topping is brown and the shrimp are cooked,
about 10 to 15 minutes, maybe longer depending on
the oven.

Serve immediately with fresh lemon. Fresh spinach
is an excellent accompaniment to this dish.

Serves two appetizers or one large entree

CAPELLINI
WITH OLIVE OIL AND GARLIC

10 oz. capellini
20 cloves of garlic
½ C. extra-virgin olive
oil, enough to sauté garlic
1½ C. chicken stock,
vegetable stock, or water
¼ C. grated cheese

1 oz. fresh chopped
parsley (or ½ bunch)
Salt to taste
Fresh ground black
pepper to taste
Crushed red pepper
flakes to taste

Lightly brown the garlic in the olive oil.

Set aside and after it's cool, add the stock or water.

Boil the water for the pasta before adding the pasta.

Bring the garlic, oil, and stock mixture to a boil.

Cook the capellini for 2 minutes, then drain.

Add the pasta to the garlic stock mixture and finish cooking, about 5 minutes or until most of the liquid is absorbed.

Finish with the grated cheese and chopped parsley; season with salt and peppers to taste.

Serve immediately.

Serves two entrees or four appetizers

155

CHOCOLATE CREME BRULEE

4 large egg yolks
2 C. heavy cream
3 oz. of sugar
1 oz. of cocoa

2 oz. of semi-sweet
chocolate, chopped
Light brown sugar for
sprinkling

Bring cream to a boil, then remove it from heat.

Stir in all ingredients, mix well, *but do not whip.*

Pour mix into 4 oven-proof cups (preferably low-sided). Place cups in a large baking pan. Add enough water to come half way up the sides of cups.

Bake in a 300° oven for about 1½ hours.

Let cool and refrigerate overnight.

Before serving, spread a light coating of brown sugar on top and brown in very hot broiler; serve.

Serves four

The regular colonial Saturday dinner was salted codfish; fish was not eaten on Fridays because to do so would acknowledge the papacy's prohibition.

156

Westbrook

This community was settled in 1648 as Pochoug, an Indian word meaning "at the confluence of two rivers", the Pochoug and the Menunketesuck, by residents of the Saybrook Colony.

Pochoug was the dwelling place of Obed and his tribe until 1676.

The community was incorporated as Third or West Parish in 1724 by an Act of the General Assembly.

This was the birthplace of David Bushnell, the American patriot and inventor of the sub-marine. It was visited by General George Washington in 1776 and by the Marquis de Lafayette in 1824.

Pochoug was renamed Westbrook in 1810 and incorporated as a town by Act of the Connecticut General Assembly in 1840.

WATER'S EDGE

1525 Boston Post Rd., Westbound
(860) 399-5901

Water's Edge is the continental restaurant at Water's Edge Resort and Country Club, a resort time-share and conference center. The restaurant is open to the public.

The facility sits on a bluff that rises above the churning waters of Long Island Sound, affording spectacular ocean views.

The cuisine has a decidedly northern Italian accent with oil based light sauces and an emphasis on Mediterranean style vegetables.

Water's Edge strikes an interesting balance: the atmosphere is quietly sophisticated but with a sophistication that recognizes that many guests are there with their families.

But something magical seems to happen to even the children while visiting *Water's Edge*: they seem to just naturally, without undue coaxing, become more subdued when dining in one of the three tiered dining areas allowing guests of all generations to drink in the mesmerizing scenery while enjoying their meals.

The Sunday Brunch Buffet may be all the excuse you need to come to the *Water's Edge*.

ZUPPA DI CLAMS POSILLIPO

6 little neck clams,
extra-small
3 cloves garlic, sliced
paper thin
3 T. extra virgin olive oil
3 oz. marinara (made with
imported Italian tomatoes)
¼ C. clam juice

3 oz. rich chicken stock
5 large leaves of fresh
basil chiffonade
Salt and pepper, to taste
Italian parsley, chopped,
to garnish

Heat the oil in a sauté pan.

Add the garlic and brown but *do not burn.*

Add the clams to the oil and garlic.

Add the marinara, clam juice, stock, basil, and salt
and pepper.

Cover and simmer on medium heat for 5 minutes or
until the clams are open.

Do not over-reduce. The sauce should be light
and brothy.

Garnish with the parsley and serve.

Serves one

FETTUCCINE ARRABBIATA
(Angry Fettuccine)

6 jumbo gulf shrimp, peeled and deveined
3 T. extra virgin olive oil
3 cloves garlic, sliced paper thin
5 oz. marinara
2 T. chicken stock
2 oz. proscuitto di Parma, sliced thin, then cut into strips
1 oz. porcini mushrooms, diced *(use dried mush-rooms, then re-hydrate in water, reserve the water)*
½ oz. porcini juice *(water used to re-hydrate the porcini)*
4 large basil leaves, chiffonade
½ t. crushed red pepper
8 oz. fettuccine, cooked al dente
Fresh parsley
Pecorino Romano

Heat the oil in a skillet pan; brown the sliced garlic in the oil. Add the marinara. (Thin out the sauce as needed with the chicken stock.)

Add the proscuitto, mushrooms, and porcini juice. Season with fresh basil and crushed red pepper.

Add shrimp to sauce, reduce heat to simmer. *Do not over-reduce.* At serving time, remove the shrimp from sauce, and add hot pasta to skillet with the sauce. Coat the pasta well with sauce.

Plate pasta and arrange shrimp. Garnish with fresh parsley and pecorino Romano.

Serves one

BILL'S SEAFOOD
548 Boston Post Rd., Westbrook
(860) 399-7224

Bill's Seafood is located at what the locals call the 'Singing Bridge" on the Boston Post Road. The place has moved back and forth on the same block some three times during its history since it was established in the 1940s. But present owner Butch Clafferty plans on keeping it right where it is.

Bill's menu is wide-ranging: from traditional fried and broiled seafood to steaks, Yankee pot roast and mahi mahi, there is certainly a choice that will appeal to everyone.

Bill's is known as much for its live entertainment as it is for its cuisine, so a call to check out the music schedule is worth the effort. The atmosphere is exceedingly informal because *Bill's* strives for a "fun, not stuffy atmosphere."

Nature lovers will enjoy dining on the deck observing the ducks and gulls. If the timing is right, diners may be lucky and spy the ospry family that nests in the marsh; they return every March and remain until early fall.

About *Bill's Seafood*, Butch says, "I always say, 'It's not my place, the people make it what it is; we just manage it.'"

SAUTÉED SOFT SHELL CRAB

Soft shell crab*
Flour for dredging
1 T. butter
Fresh chopped garlic, to taste
Juice of ¼ lemon

2 capers
Salt to taste
Toasted bun or toast points
Tomato garnish

* If possible, use a fresh soft shell crab; however, frozen is acceptable. If the crab is frozen, allow it to thaw naturally in the refrigerator. *Do not put it in water or in the microwave oven.*

Under running cool water, reach into the center of the crab and clean out the green substance in the chest cavity. Rinse it out well. *Be very gentle because the legs are fragile.*

Flour the damp soft shell crab. In a sauté pan, add the butter, garlic, lemon juice, capers, and salt and heat on high. When the pan is hot, add the crab and cook it for about 1½ minutes, flip it and cook for another 1½ minutes or until the crab is pinkish'.

Season or not, depending on taste. Drizzle the pan dressing on top of the crab and serve it on a toasted bun or toast points with a tomato garnish and a vegetable.

Serves one

BLUE CHEESE CHICKEN

4 oz. boneless chicken
breast
Butter for sautéing
Garlic powder
Salt and pepper to taste

Italian seasoning, *optional*
¼ C. sliced mushrooms
3 T. blue cheese dressing
Provolone cheese slices*
*or Swiss or Muenster

Clean and rinse the chicken breast well.

Season the chicken with the garlic powder, salt and pepper, and Italian seasoning, if using.

Heat the butter in a sauté pan and add the chicken.

Sauté lightly until both sides are golden brown.

Remove the chicken to a baking dish.

In the same pan, sauté the mushrooms.

Top the chicken with the mushrooms.

Spread your favorite blue cheese dressing on the mushrooms and top it all with the cheese slices.

Cook in a quick 400° oven until the cheese is melted and the chicken is thoroughly cooked.

Serves one

Say-Brooke

Founded November 1635. First English settlement on south shore of New England.

Named for Viscount Say and Seal and Robert, Lord Brooke, two of the group of English nobility and gentry who, in 1632, received a patent from Robert, Earl of Warwick, to lands from the Narragansett River to the Pacific Ocean.

A fort was established at the mouth of the Connecticut River to protect it for English colonists.

First church was organized in 1646 in the fort's Great Hall. Fourth edifice, built 1840, stands opposite. Many nearby homes sprang from Say-Brooke.

The site of the original colony is now called Old Saybrook.

TERRA MAR GRILLE
at The Saybrook Point Inn and Spa, 2 Bridge St., Old Saybrook
(860) 395-2000

Terra Mar Grille at The Saybrook Point Inn & Spa overlooks a 125 slip marina on Long Island Sound. The 62 suite Inn and conference center provides spa services (facials, manicures, pedicures and massages) and a fitness center for its guests. But if culinary indulgence is on your menu, the *Terra Mar Grille* is for you.

Executive Chef Brian J. Alberg says his goal is to serve attractively presented, sophisticated fare that is worthy of the finest Manhattan restaurant — but without the high prices. The menu changes seasonally to optimize ingredient availability and freshness. Brian even grows heirloom seeds for herbs like pineapple basil in his own garden near the restaurant.

Intrepid diners should know that the *Terra Mar Grille* has presented six course wine tasting dinners and Wild Game Nights during the off-season. The latter has featured such unusual delicacies as wild boar, bear, and musk ox.

A pictorial history of the Inn is displayed along the hallway; the site has been a resort destination since 1870 and the restaurant is named for the original hotel, the Terra Mar.

PAN SEARED FOIE GRAS WITH CARAMELIZED APPLES AND CROSTINI

6 oz. Grade 'A' Foie Gras (Slice into four ½" slices; *keep very cold)*

CARAMELIZED APPLES

2 Granny Smith apples	**Pinch of coriander**
1 T. butter	**¼ C. currants**

Peel and dice the apples.

Melt the butter until it is golden brown.

Add the apples, coriander, and currants.

Sauté the mixture until caramel in color but not too soft.

Reserve on the side, keeping warm.

1 bunch arugula	**1 t. olive oil**	**1 T. balsamic vinegar**

Wash the greens thoroughly.

Julienne into long strips.

Dress with olive oil and balsamic vinegar.

(Continued...)

*PAN SEARED FOIE GRAS WITH CARAMELIZED
APPLES AND CROSTINI (...continued)*

CROSTINI

**4 slices country-style
bread**

1 T. olive oil

Remove the crust from the bread.

Brush with the olive oil.

Lightly toast in the oven.

ASSEMBLY

Using no oil, sear the Foie Gras in a hot pan for
about 60 seconds on each side.

Put a couple of tablespoons of the apple mixture
on the plate.

Top it with a crostini.

Top the crostini with a slice of the seared Foie Gras.

Place a nice pile of the julienned arugula on top of it all.

Serves four

167

PROSCIUTTO WRAPPED PORK TENDERLOIN WITH WHITE POLENTA AND SUMMER RATATOUILLE

2 pork tenderloins (about 1 lb.)
2 garlic cloves, chopped
1 T. chopped rosemary
Salt and pepper
10-12 slices of Parma prosciutto
1 T. olive oil

Season the pork with the garlic, rosemary, and salt and pepper. Layer half of the prosciutto slices width-wise.

Place the tenderloin on the bottom edge and roll it up away from you. Repeat with the remaining prosciutto and tenderloin.

With 1 T. of olive oil in a hot pan, sear the pork until it is golden on all sides.

Remove it from the burner and finish in a 350° oven for about 20 minutes.

WHITE POLENTA

½ C. yellow or white polenta (corn meal)
2 C. whole milk
Salt and pepper
1 T. butter

Bring the milk to a boil without scalding it.

Add the salt, pepper, and butter. *(Continued...)*

168

Sprinkle the polenta over the top of the milk, stirring it so it won't lump. Reduce the heat to low and cook until the polenta starts to pull away from the sides of the pot.

SUMMER RATATOUILLE

½ zucchini
½ yellow squash
½ red pepper
½ red onion
1 T. garlic

1 plum tomato
¼ C. diced basil
2 T. olive oil
Salt and pepper

Small dice all of the vegetables, then sauté the zucchini, squash, peppers, onions, and garlic in the oil until slightly soft.

Add the tomatoes, basil, salt and pepper and cook for another 5 minutes.

ASSEMBLY

Slice the pork into 8 slices per tenderloin; put the polenta in the center of the plate, then the Ratatouille on the top half of the plate.

At the bottom of the plate, fan the pork slices around the polenta.

Serves four

169

LIME POT AU CREME

1 quart cream   12 egg yolks, beaten
¾ C. sugar   1 lime leaf
1 t. vanilla

Bring the cream, sugar, and vanilla to a boil.

Carefully add half of the mixture into the yolks.

Mix the yolks back into the remaining cream.

This is called tempering and it is done to make sure the yolks do not scramble.

Add the lime leaf and let it sit for about 10 minutes.

Remove the leaf and pour the mixture into shallow baking dishes or a shallow souffle dish.

Cook in a water bath at 325° until firm to the touch, about 20 to 30 minutes.

Serves eight

William Fiennes, Lord Say and Sele, was a member of Parliament and a firm exponent of the abolishment of Episcopacy and a leading advocate of Presbyterianism.

DOCK & DINE
Saybrook Point, Old Saybrook
(860) 388-4665

The name *Dock & Dine* leaves no doubt that it is ideally situated for boaters. Located smack dab at the intersection of the Connecticut River and Long Island Sound, this casual, bright and airy establishment is open for lunch and dinner and it is large enough to accommodate diners in its dining rooms plus 180 people in its banquet room.

Chef Bill Geary says locals can't remember a time when there wasn't an eatery named *Dock & Dine* here; the present owners have been pleasing diners for the last twelve years.

When it comes to food, Bill said, "We offer fresh, well-prepared food. Consistency is the key to our menu. If you enjoy a particular dish, you can feel sure you'll enjoy it during your next visit."

Dock & Dine is open daily during the high season (Easter through Columbus Day) and Wednesday through Sunday from Columbus Day to Easter.

For those looking for more than great seafood, Bill wants you to know that *Dock & Dine's* menu also features Angus beef, pasta and chicken specials nightly.

171

CALALLOO CRAB MEAT SOUP

½ onion, finely diced
4 T. olive oil
2 cloves garlic, minced
1 bay leaf
2 qts. heavy cream
10 oz. can chicken consomme

13 oz. can coconut milk
1 C. coarsely chopped spinach, stems removed
8 oz. crab meat
Salt
White pepper to taste

Sauté the onions in olive oil over medium heat until translucent. Add the garlic and sauté for 1 minute longer. Add the bay leaf.

Stir in the heavy cream, chicken consomme, and coconut milk to combine. Reduce over medium-high heat until it is the consistency of a cream soup (20 to 60 minutes depending on the level of heat under the pot), stirring frequently and taking care not to let soup boil over. Reduce heat.

In a separate pan, drop the spinach into boiling water and drain immediately.

Add spinach to the soup and then the crab meat, just to heat through. Season to taste with salt and white pepper. Remove the bay leaf.

Serve while hot.

Serves eight

172

BLUEFISH STEAMED IN A TOMATO SAFFRON BROTH WITH MUSSELS AND CLAMS

4 bluefish filets (6-8 oz. each)
12 mussels, de-bearded and washed
12 little neck clams, washed
Tomato Saffron Broth

TOMATO SAFFRON BROTH

¼ C. olive oil
½ onion, sliced
1 medium leek, cut in
half, washed and sliced
1 oz. garlic, chopped
½ T. chopped tarragon
½ T. chopped basil
½ T. fennel seed, lightly
crushed

2 bay leaves
¾ C. crushed tomatoes
12 oz. canned peeled
plum tomatoes, pureed
Pinch saffron
2½ qt. fish stock
Black pepper
Kosher salt

Sauté onions, leeks, garlic, tarragon, basil and fennel together in the oil until the onions and leeks are soft.

Add the bay leaves, tomato products, and saffron.

Simmer for 5 minutes, stirring.

Add the fish stock and bring to a boil.

Simmer for about 30 minutes. Season to taste. Remove the bay leaves.

Note: Best if made day before.   *(Continued...)*

173

ASSEMBLY

Season and place the bluefish filets in a 9" x 11" stove-top-safe shallow pan.

Pour the broth over the filets, just to cover them.

Making sure that the onions and leeks are on top of the filets, place the clams and mussels around the edge of the pan.

Bring to a boil on the top of the stove.

Cover with aluminum foil.

Place in a 350° oven for approximately 15 to 20 minutes or until the fish is done.

Place bluefish filets in the center of each plate.

Arrange the shellfish around the filet. Ladle some broth on the fish and serve.

Serves four

Dock & Dine's recipes were created by Chef Bill Geary

BLACKENED STRIPED BASS
WITH COCONUT FLAVORED BASMATI RICE, YELLOW VINE RIPENED TOMATO SALSA AND RED PEPPER COULIS

COCONUT FLAVORED BASMATI RICE

¾ C. basmati rice
¼ C. water
½ C. unsweetened coconut milk
½ bay leaf

Combine all ingredients together in a pan and then bring to a boil. Cover the pan. Reduce to simmer and cook until the rice is tender. Remove the bay leaf.

STRIPED BASS

6 (2 oz. each) medallions of striped bass
Cajun spice
Oil for pan

Lightly coat 1 side only of the bass in the Cajun spice.

Heat a cast iron pan on high.

Lightly coat the bottom with oil.

Blacken the fish in the pan.

Turn over when spiced side has a nice crust.

(Continued...)

175

YELLOW VINE RIPENED TOMATO SALSA

½ C. yellow vine-ripe tomatoes, peeled, seeded and diced
3 t. finely diced red onions

1 t. fresh lime juice
1 t. fresh lemon juice
½ t. finely diced jalepeño
Pinch salt
1 t. diced cilantro

Combine all of the ingredients together in a stainless steel bowl. Refrigerator at least 1 hour before serving.

RED PEPPER COULIS

2 red peppers, cut in half and seeded
¼ C. white wine
¼ of a shallot

½ bay leaf
¼ t. cracked black peppercorns
½ C. chicken stock

Reduce the wine, shallot, bay leaf, and peppercorns by half. Add the red peppers and chicken stock.

Bring to a boil. Cover and reduce to simmer and cook until the peppers are soft. Remove bay leaf.

Puree in a food processor. Pass through large hole sieve.

Season to taste.

(Continued...)

ASSEMBLY

Garnish:

**Carrot curls
Chopped purple kale**

Place a pool of coulis on a plate.

Set the rice in the center of the plate.

Arrange 3 medallions of fish around the rice.

Place the salsa on top.

Garnish with carrot curls and chopped purple kale.

Serve with appropriate vegetable.

Serves two

Robert, Lord Brook, was a member of Parliament and a colleague of Lord Say and Sele. Both lords advocated religious freedom.

Niantic/East Lyme

Settled in the 1640s in part of Lyme and New London, East Lyme was made a separate town in 1839 by the Connecticut General Assembly.

In what was originally a farming area along the Old Post Road, a cottage textile industry developed similar to that in Belgium, which gained for the district the name Flanders.

Prior to the arrival of the settlers, the Nehantic Indians fished and hunted along the shoreline, and afterward lived among the newcomers who gave this district its name of Niantic, a variant of the tribal name. The Thomas Lee House (1660) and the Smith Harris House (1840) are both fine examples of the architecture of their time. A plaque at Bride Brook on Route 156 tells of a romantic marriage there in 1646 and marks the boundary between what was then Saybrook and New London. The town now encompasses 34.8 square miles. Today Niantic is part of East Lyme as are Flanders and Nehantic.

CONSTANTINE'S
252 Main St., Niantic
(860) 739-2848

Constantine's has the distinction of being the longest family-owned and operated restaurant in New London County. Seventy years ago, present owner Andy Pappas's grandfather founded the restaurant and over the years it has evolved into a favorite neighborhood kind-of-place. As Andy says, "Long before there was a 'Cheers', there was *Constantine's*. You can come in on a Friday or Saturday night and you'll notice that almost everyone seems to know each other. This is the place where the natives come; they find us by word of mouth."

Some customers have been dining here for 30 years. The staff stays for years and many have encouraged their relatives to join them at *Constantine's*.

History permeates *Constantine's* and history buffs won't want to miss the photos of Niantic's past that grace the walls.

Chef Alan Stewart says it best: "Come in and see the same friendly faces you saw last time — and you can be sure you'll receive the same quality food and service day in and day out year round. Consistency is the key here; it really is."

GREEK CHICKEN SAUTÉ

6 boneless, skinless chicken breasts, cut in half
1 C. flour for dredging
1 t. salt
1 t. black pepper
½ C. olive oil
2 C. mushrooms, sliced
1 C. shallots, sliced

2 t. chopped fresh rosemary
6 t. fresh oregano, whole
1 C. white wine
36 calamata olives, pitted
24 sun dried tomatoes, cut in half
1 C. feta cheese

Season the flour with salt and pepper, then dredge the chicken in the flour.

Heat the oil in a skillet.

When the oil is hot, add 2 of the chicken breasts. Brown the chicken on both sides, then remove and set aside as you finish browning the rest of the chicken, continuing to brown 2 at a time.

Return the chicken to the skillet and add the mushrooms, shallots, rosemary, and oregano.

Cook for 2 minutes or until the mushrooms start to get soft, then add the wine, olives, sun dried tomatoes, and feta cheese. Cook 1 more minute or until chicken is cooked through.

Serves six

CLAMS BOURSIN

24 little neck clams
Oil for sautéing
12 shallots, peeled and
diced
2 red bell peppers, diced
10 oz. package of frozen
spinach (thawed)

3 (4 oz.) packages of
Boursin cheese*
Bread crumbs
  *Boursin cheese can be
purchased at most major
supermarkets and
gourmet food stores.

Pre-heat the oven to 350°.

Shuck open the clams. Leave them on the half shell.

Sauté the shallots and peppers until they are translucent, then set them aside.

Arrange the clams in a shallow baking pan.

Top each clam with 2 t. of spinach and 2 t. of
the shallot and pepper mixture.

Bake for 15 minutes at 350°.

Remove from the oven and top with 1 T. of Boursin
cheese and sprinkle the bread crumbs on top and
bake for 3 to 5 more minutes.

Serves six

APPLE CRISP

10 Granny Smith apples   ⅔ C. flour
1 T. white sugar   ½ C. light brown sugar
1 T. cinnamon   ½ lb. butter, softened

Pre-heat the oven to 350°.

Peel, core, and slice the apples.

Sprinkle the apples with the white sugar and cinnamon. Toss.

Coat a shallow 13" x 9" baking pan with butter.

Put the apples in the pan.

Next, mix the flour and brown sugar together.

Add the butter and mix it together until the mixture is crumbly.

Put the mixture on top of the apples.

Bake for 45 minutes to 1 hour or until the apples are soft and the topping is light brown.

Serves twelve

Constantine's recipes created by Alan Stewart

MANGIA MANGIA
215 Main St., Niantic
(860) 739-9074

Mangia Mangia's owner, Billy Frausini, used to visit his Italian grandparents during the summer. Although his grandmother didn't speak much English, it was she who taught him how to cook. The restaurant got its name from her loving admonitions to him to 'mangia, mangia, buon, buon': eat, eat, good, good.

And that's the same message this entrepreneur gives to his patrons: "Come and eat good food." Seafood, steaks, and more, all with an Italian flare.

The building, known as the Morton House, has been completely renovated with a nautical theme. (Originally a summer house with an underground tunnel to the beach.) Billy's dad was a musician and when he accompanied him to clubs he would hang around in the kitchen while his father was playing. For as long as he can remember he's only wanted to be in the restaurant business.

Mangia Mangia has two dining rooms; windows over-look the water. The daily lunch buffet makes a stop here a nice mid-day treat and for those looking for humor, it's the new home of Treehouse Comedy Productions.

PASSATELLI SOUP

1 lemon	2 C. bread crumbs
3 eggs	Salt and pepper to taste
1 C. grated Parmesan or Asiago cheese	3 qts. chicken broth

Grate the lemon's rind into the eggs.

Whisk together.

Add the grated cheese, bread crumbs, and salt and pepper.

Mix well and form into balls.

Remove the cutting wheel from a meat grinder.

Put the balls through the meat grinder using the extruder that will form fat spaghetti shaped strands.

Put the chicken broth into a soup pot and bring it to a boil.

Add the noodles and continue to let the pot boil for 5 to 7 minutes.

Serves nine

CAESAR DRESSING

2 C. olive oil
Juice of 2 lemons
1½ T. chopped garlic
½ T. Worcestershire
sauce

½ tube anchovy paste
8 egg yolks*
½ T. black pepper
1 C. grated Asiago or
Parmesan cheese

You may want to use an Egg Substitute to avoid risks associated with raw eggs and salmonella

Put all of the ingredients, *except the cheese*, into a food processor.

Whip on medium for 2 minutes.

Add the cheese and mix by hand.

Refrigerate overnight.

Mix again when ready to use.

Pour some dressing over romaine lettuce and serve.

Yields one pint

Puritan men disliked long hair and a bowl or half pumpkin shell was often used to achieve the right look.

Waterford

Incorporated 1801.

English colonists first harvested crops on Fog Plain and Mamacoke in 1645, gradually displacing the native Nehantic and Pequot Indians.

Farm lots were allocated to individual colonists in 1651 and in 1653 a sawmill site and house lot were designated on Hunts Brook in Quaker Hill. The Jordan area was first mentioned in 1663 and Jordan Schoolhouse in 1737.

Waterford gave thousands of acres to help form East Lyme in 1899 and two square miles were taken for New London by legislative action in 1899, leaving the present area of 36.7 square miles.

UNK'S ON THE BAY
361 Rope Ferry Rd., Waterford
(860) 443-2717

Unk's was owned before WWII by Mr. Denison, whose nickname was 'unk'. In 1963 when Martha and Roland Bouffard bought the business, then a clam bar, they kept the name, but everything else has this family's mark. As the business grew, Roland literally banged every nail for each addition until his retirement.

Fishermen note: An impressive white marlin caught by Roland in 1968 off Montauk Point is mounted on the wall; its likeness has become *Unk's* logo.

Still family operated, Suzanne and David bring a creative and innovative style to *Unk's*. Specializing in fresh seafood but not limited to that, *Unk's* provides petite and regular size portions; heart healthy entrees; and a traditional roast dinner every Sunday (for under $10).

While the deck closes after the summer season, year-round dining brings changes with the seasons. Theme menus start with Harvest Festival; Oktoberfest; Dickens; and Spring Festival. *Unk's* uses authentic recipes to create traditional fare for each theme — giving you at least four more reasons to stop by *Unk's on the Bay* — as if the water views weren't enough.

SEAFOOD LASAGNE

1 lb. scallop pieces
1 lb. shrimp pieces
1 lbs. crab meat (snow, rock or imitation)
1 box cooked lasagna sheets
1 pint ricotta cheese
1 pint cottage cheese
2 t. chopped garlic
½ t. oregano

½ t. basil
¼ t. red pepper flakes
Salt and pepper to taste
1 lb. Parmesan cheese, shredded
1 lb. Provolone cheese, shredded
1 jar al Fredo sauce (store bought)

Spray a 10" x 15" deep casserole pan with non-stick spray.

Mix the seafood with the ricotta and cottage cheeses, garlic, and spices.

Blend the Parmesan and Provolone cheeses together.

Assemble the lasagna starting with a thin layer of al Fredo sauce, then pasta sheets, followed by a layer of the seafood mix, followed by the shredded cheeses.

Repeat these steps 2 more times; finish with a layer of pasta sheets, then cheese; cover with aluminum foil.

Bake at 350° for 1 hour, or until thermometer reads 160°; cool for 30 minutes before cutting.

SEAFOOD STIR FRY

1 lb. medium shrimp
½ lb. scallops
1 lb. white flaky cod fish
½ lb. salmon
1 T. sesame oil
1 T. sesame seeds
Snow peas
Broccoli florets
1 carrot, peeled and cut
into ½" thick pieces

Green pepper strips
Red pepper strips
Chopped onion
Zucchini, cut into half
moons
1 T. chopped garlic
3 T. DeFelice teriyaki
sauce (store bought)
Cooked white rice
Scallions, chopped

Heat the sesame oil.

Sauté the seafood pieces until flaky.

Add the sesame seeds, vegetables, and garlic.

After about 3 minutes, add the teriyaki sauce.

Cook for another 2 minutes.

Serve over cooked white rice and garnish with
fresh scallions.

Serves four

189

CARROT CAKE
WITH CREAM CHEESE FROSTING

3 C. unbleached all-
purpose flour
3 C. granulated sugar
1 t. salt
1 T. baking soda
1 T. cinnamon
1½ C. corn oil
4 large eggs

1 T. vanilla extract
1½ C. walnuts, shelled
and chopped
1½ C. shredded coconut
11 oz. pureed cooked
carrots
¾ C. drained crushed
pineapple

Preheat the oven to 350° (325° for convection oven).
Grease two 9" layer cake pans and dust with flour.

Sift dry ingredients into a bowl. Add the oil, eggs,
and vanilla. Beat well. Reserve some of the walnuts,
then fold in the remaining walnuts and the coconut,
carrots, and pineapple.

Pour into the prepared pans. Set on middle rack of
the oven. Bake for 35 to 55 minutes, until edges pull
away from sides and cake tester comes out clean.

Cool cake on rack for 3 hours.

Fill cake with Cream Cheese Frosting; cover sides
and top with frosting.

Sprinkle top with chopped walnuts.

(Continued...)

190

CREAM CHEESE FROSTING

16 oz. cream cheese
6 T. sweet butter
4 - 5 C. confectioners sugar, sifted
1 t. vanilla

Cream together the cream cheese and butter in a mixing bowl until it is smooth.

Slowly add the sifted sugar and continue beating until it is fully incorporated.

Stir in the vanilla.

The nearest an English throat could make to the Indian word for "the long river" was probably about kwon-egh-te-kut; the second syllable representing a very rough and harsh guttural sound has no counter-part in English and in writing it was represented by the English guttural available in the 'k' sound.

191

SUNSET RIB CO.
378 Rope Ferry Rd., Waterford
(860) 443-RIBS (7427)

Sunset Ribs is a rustic, versatile, upbeat restaurant with a green and brass decor that, yes, specializes in ribs.

Manager Carol Dion says the meat on their ribs "just falls off the bones" and "people come from as far as New York just for the ribs." Even the CIA wouldn't be able to get them to disclose their secrets, but Carol will say that the preparation includes rubbing with spices, a special smoker, steaming, and quick grilling. While 75 percent of the diners order ribs, the menu offers "a little bit of everything else, too."

Sunset Ribs is also where bikers, children, and grandparents rub shoulders and "let their hair down", especially on Sundays. Weekend entertainment is a key ingredient here, with the billing changing as the day matures: A soloist or acoustic duo is usually performing on the deck during the day; after 10 p.m., the volume increases as the lounge is transformed into a nightclub.

If you come late in the day, Carol says you'll see the "most fantastic sunsets" as that celestial body makes its journey across the sky — so be sure to have your camera. (Seasonal)

PACHOS

8 oz. cream cheese	1 t. pepper
1 T. oregano	1 t. salt
1 T. basil	

Mix together in an oven-safe casserole dish.

¼ C. diced peppers	¼ C. diced jalapeños
¼ C. diced onions	¼ C. diced pepperoni

Marinara sauce
Shredded Mozzarella cheese
Tortilla chips

Blend together the peppers, onions, jalapeños, and the pepperoni.

Cover the cream cheese mixture with this topping.

Top with your favorite marinara sauce, enough to cover the top.

Cover with the shredded mozzarella cheese.

Bake at 375° for 10 minutes or until bubbly.

Serve with your favorite tortilla chips.

Serves four

SUNSET PASTA*

Angel hair pasta, cooked
Chicken breast, seasoned
with Cajun spices or
lemon pepper, if desired

Romaine lettuce,
shredded
Caesar dressing, bottled
Parmesan cheese

*Determine quantities of ingredients according to
number being served and preferences*

Grill the chicken breast and cook enough angel hair
pasta per person.

While the pasta is cooking, toss the romaine lettuce
with your favorite Caesar dressing and Parmesan
cheese (enough for your own liking).

Toss the drained pasta with some Caesar dressing
and Parmesan cheese to moisten the pasta.

Place the pasta on top of the salad.

Slice the chicken breast and place the slices on top of
the pasta and enjoy!

---

*It may have been disingenuous, but by the
middle of the 18th Century, Connecticut
claimed it was feeling over-populated;
population: 133,000*

194

NIANTIC BAY PASTA

1 lb. of angel hair pasta, cooked, drained, and chilled
1½ lbs. bay scallops
Flour for dredging
Olive oil for sautéing
12 oz. sun dried tomatoes
4 t. minced garlic

1½ C. button mushrooms, sliced
1 T. dried parsley
¼ C. chopped shallots
2 C. heavy cream
1 C. grated Parmesan cheese
Garlic bread

Coat the scallops with the flour.

Sauté them in the olive oil in a sauté pan over medium heat until they are golden brown.

Add the sun dried tomatoes, garlic, sliced mushrooms, parsley, and the shallots.

Sauté until the sun dried tomatoes are soft.

Add the heavy cream and let it reduce by half.

Add the cup of Parmesan cheese.

Toss the mixture with the angel hair pasta and serve with the garlic bread.

Serves four

New London

New London was founded in 1646 by John Winthrop, the younger, who chose this shore-ringed "plantation" for its excellent harbor.

This land, with its great natural assets, attracted men of hardihood and valor and became one of the largest whaling ports in the country in the mid-19th century.

As this industry waned, manufacturing flourished, bringing an influx of foreign labor which contributed immeasurably to the enrichment of community life.

The history of New London may be said to be concentrated in its seal, adopted when the city was incorporated in 1784: a full-rigged ship with all sails set and the motto "Mare Liberum", meaning "Freedom of the Seas".

THE UPPER DECK
130 Pequot Ave., New London
(860) 439-0884

At the *Upper Deck*, officially the Upper
Deck Restaurant and School of Cooking,
owner and chef Chuck Moran has found a way
to blend his two loves, cooking and teaching.
The classically trained chef got his career start
in an unusual way: he joined the Navy and
spent four years as the cook on a submarine,
receiving commendations from the command
for his cooking expertise. The experience
encouraged him to attend the Culinary Institute of America. A chance to teach awakened a
desire to share his culinary skills with others.

The result is an establishment that is half
restaurant (125 seats) and half display kitchen.
He notes that both sides are visible to the
other which makes it a unique space. The
diningroom windows overlook Green Harbor
Beach.

Chuck says his cooking "reaches down
to the depths of classical cooking," but with a
regional flair. All of the desserts, chowders, and
soups are homemade. Cheesecake aficionados
beware: Chuck changes the flavor of the always
available cheesecake according to his mood —
it may be banana rum, cranberry kaluha, or
peach frangelica — or something entirely new.

CREAM OF CARROT CARAWAY SOUP

2 lbs. carrots, peeled and sliced
2½ qts. chicken stock or broth
1 C. onions, medium dice
2 ribs celery, medium dice
¼ C. golden sherry
1 T. caraway seeds
¼ C. honey
Pinch of thyme
2 bay leaves
White pepper to taste
¾ C. half and half or heavy cream

Prepare the vegetables as specified and place them in a soup pot.

Cover with the stock and bring to a boil.

Add the remaining ingredients, *except the cream.*

Simmer approximately 40 minutes or until the carrots are tender.

Remove the bay leaves, then puree in a blender or food processor.

Adjust the seasoning and finish with the cream.

Yields three quarts, ten to twelve servings

ROAST DUCKLING WITH APRICOTS, ALMONDS, AND AMARETTO

2 (4-4½ lb.) ducklings
Soy sauce
2 C. apricot nectar
About ¾ C. brown
sugar, as needed

¼ C. Amaretto
Cornstarch dissolved in
cold water
1 can apricot halves
2-3 oz. toasted almonds

Rub the ducks with soy sauce and prick with a large fork or pointed knife.

Roast in a 450° oven for about 30 minutes, until golden brown.

Reduce the heat to 350° and roast for 1 hour.

Remove the ducks from the oven and cool; remove the meat from the carcass.

SAUCE

Bring the apricot nectar, brown sugar, and Amaretto to a boil. Add the dissolved cornstarch to the liquid slowly, until it will coat a spoon.

Heat the apricot halves. Reheat the meat in a moderate oven for 12 to 15 minutes. Place on a platter and top with the apricots. Top with the sauce and garnish with toasted almonds.

Serves four

PUMPKIN CHEESECAKE

2½ lbs. cream cheese	½ t. ginger
(at room temperature)	¼ t. cloves
2 large egg yolks	¼ t. allspice
5 large eggs	2 pinches of cardamom
3 T. flour	Pinch of salt
1¾ C. sugar	1½ C. pumpkin
¾ t. cinnamon	¾ C. bourbon

Combine the sugar with the flour.

In the mixer, beat the cream cheese smooth. Add the eggs and mix.

Add the sugar mixture and spices (mixed together). Blend to incorporate, then add the pumpkin and bourbon; blend well.

Butter the sides of a 3" x 9" round cake pan; coat with sugar. Add 2 parchment disks with non-stick spray in-between. Pour in cake batter.

Place into a water bath and bake in a 350° oven for 1 hour and 15 minutes.

Remove cake pan from water bath and place on metal rack to cool. Refrigerate overnight in the pan before turning onto a serving plate. Serve.

Serves sixteen

200

THE LIGHTHOUSE INN
6 Guthrie Pl., New London
(860) 443-8411

Built in 1902, the *Lighthouse Inn* was originally the steel magnate Charles Guthrie's country home, Meadow Court, overlooking Long Island Sound. The formal grounds were designed by landscape architect Fredrick Olmsted, who also designed Central Park. The Mediterranean style mansion formed a half circle so every room of the house had a view of the gardens or Long Island Sound. It has been operated as an inn since 1927; its mansion guest rooms are filled with antiques, four-poster beds, and armoires.

The restaurant is described by its Executive Chef, Sean Mirsky, as "more upscale with eclectic continental fare with a different twist." Sean, a Johnson and Wales graduate, brings an artist's eye for 3-dimensional design to his gustatory creations, believing dining should intrigue all of the senses.

Many of the mansion's rooms are used for dining: There are multiple dining rooms plus a wood paneled smoking lounge and terrace. Off season, the glow from the fireplaces add to the cozy ambience. At least for a little while, you can indulge your fancy at *The Lighthouse Inn* and pretend that this is your country house.

SWEET DUMPLING SQUASH SOUP WITH CRISPY SWEET POTATO PIECES

5 sweet dumpling squashes, *tops cut off and seeds removed*	1 small Spanish onion, chopped
5 t. olive oil	2 C. water
Salt and pepper	Crispy sweet potato pieces
2 T. butter	2 t. chopped chervil

Season the inside of the squashes with olive oil, salt, and pepper.

Place cut side down on a sheet tray and pour a ½" of water on the tray.

Bake at 375° for 1 hour or until squashes are tender.

Remove from oven and completely scrape out the pulp of 1 squash, discarding the skin.

Scrape the pulp out of the 4 remaining squashes, leaving ¼" of the flesh adhered to the skin.

Sweat the onions in the butter in a small sauté pan over medium heat until translucent.

Place onions, water, and squash pulp in a blender and puree until smooth. Pass through a fine-mesh sieve and reheat in a small sauce pan.

Season to taste with salt and pepper.   *(Continued...)*

202

Place squash shells in the oven at 350° for 5 minutes.

Remove and fill with the hot soup.

ASSEMBLY

Place 1 of the squashes in the center of each plate.

Place a few of the crispy sweet potato pieces on top of the soup and arrange some around the plate.

Sprinkle with the chopped chervil.

Serves four

The Lighthouse's recipes were created by Chef Sean Mirsky

STEAMED HALIBUT AND OYSTERS WITH LEMON GRASS, BRAISED BOK CHOY, AND SOBA NOODLES

16 oysters, steamed and shucked	½ C. red satin radishes
4 C. fish stock	½ C. cucumber, julienned
2 stalks lemon grass	16 slices of water chestnuts
Salt and pepper	4 T. nori, julienned
4 (3 oz.) pieces of halibut	4 T. shiso, julienned
1 C. bok choy, chopped	½ C. chopped scallions
4 oz. cooked soba noodles	4 t. sesame oil

Blanch the bok choy and set aside.

Place the fish stock in a medium sauce pan with the lemon grass.

Simmer over medium heat for 20 minutes to infuse the stock.

Strain through a fine-mesh sieve and season to taste with salt and pepper.

Season the halibut with salt and pepper.

Place in a steamer for 3 to 5 minutes, or until just done.

Warm the blanched bok choy in the fish stock over low heat for 2 minutes.

(Continued...)

ASSEMBLY

In the center of each bowl, place some of the soba noodles, radish, and cucumber.

Place a piece of the steamed halibut on top of the noodles.

Place a slice of water chestnuts at the 4 corners of the halibut and set an oyster on top of each water chestnut.

Ladle 1 cup of the fish stock and bok choy into each bowl.

Sprinkle the nori, shiso, and scallions around the bowl.

Drizzle the sesame oil around the bowl and top with freshly ground black pepper.

Serves four

The Boston Post Road was the 'post' or mail road between New York and Boston with relay stations in Hartford and Saybrook.

Groton

As part of New London Plantation, Groton was settled in 1646 by John Winthrop, the younger, and a band of Puritans from Massachusetts. The town separated from New London in 1705, and was named for the Winthrop manor in England.

One of the last battles of the American Revolution was fought on Groton Heights at Fort Griswold, September 6, 1781. The Groton Monument commemorates the battle. A state park now preserves the fort area.

Groton is the site of the Submarine Base of the United States Navy, and home of the builder of much of the Navy's undersea fleet. It is the birthplace of the nuclear submarine.

PASTA PAUL'S SHOP
223 Thames St., Groton
(860) 445-5276

Paul and Dorothy Fidrych, the owners of *Pasta Paul's*, are truly an epicurean couple. Paul is a graduate of the Culinary Institute of America and Dorothy is an alumna of Johnson and Wales. In 1988 they opened Pasta Paul's as a fresh pasta/gourmet shop with a few tables. Very quickly, customers began asking them to add more tables. Today they can accommodate 45 diners inside and 35 on the deck.

The restaurant is located in a former store front so the hustle and bustle of the street is visible through the picture windows while diners who prefer watching the river front activity on the Thames River can have their wish, too.

There is one delightful dilemma that confronts every diner at *Pasta Paul's*: what to order. They make 20 — 30 different styles of pasta — including egg, whole wheat, spinach, black pepper, and garlic — with eight to ten varieties available daily, plus cavatelli, tortellini, and ravioli. As if that isn't enough, non-pasta choices are also available.

Paul notes that while many people associate pasta with Italian cuisine, he doesn't consider *Pasta Paul's* an Italian restaurant.

SPAGHETTI PIE

CRUST

1½ lbs. fresh spaghetti, *cooked al dente and cooled*	2 lbs. ricotta cheese 2 eggs ½ C. grated Parmesan

FILLING

6 links (hot and/or sweet) Italian sausage, *cooked and sliced*	1 C. mushrooms, sliced 1 large green pepper, sliced
1 lb. ground beef, *browned*	2 C. tomato sauce

TOPPING

¼ lb. pepperoni, sliced
½ lb. mozzarella, sliced or shredded
1½ qts. tomato sauce

ASSEMBLY

Mix the "crust" ingredients together, then spread on a lightly oiled baking pan or dish, 12" round or 9" x 12".

Mix the filling ingredients with the 2 C. of sauce and spread over the crust. Top with the pepperoni, then the mozzarella and the remaining sauce.

Bake 45 minutes in a pre-heated 350° oven.

Serves six to ten

LINGUINI PRIMAVERA

1½ lbs. fresh linguini	1 red bell pepper
1 broccoli crown	½ C. olive oil
½ cauliflower crown	½ C. white wine or
1 green squash	water
1 yellow squash	1 T. chopped garlic
½ lb. mushrooms	Salt and pepper to taste
½ C. pitted black olives	1 t. chopped parsley

Trim and slice vegetables into bite-size pieces.

In a large sauté pan combine the oil, wine, garlic, salt, and pepper.

Add the vegetables and turn on high.

Sauté vegetables until they are cooked.

Meanwhile, cook the pasta in boiling water.

Strain and add hot to the hot veggie mixture.

Add the parsley.

Mix well and serve right away.

Serves four

CREAMY GARLIC DRESSING

1 pint mayonnaise   1 t. parsley flakes
2 T. lemon juice   Salt
¼ C. water   Black pepper
2 T. chopped garlic

Combine all ingredients and mix well.

Yields 2½ cups

_____

*Pasta Paul's recipes were created
by Chef Paul Fidrych*

HARBOUR SEAL
359 Thames St., Groton
(860) 446-0051

It wasn't until after Eileen and David Gaudette named their restaurant *Harbour Seal* that Eileen swears she saw a seal sunbathing beyond the fenced deck that hovers over the Thames River as it meets Long Island Sound.

Originally Groton's Town Hall, *Harbour Seal*, with its wide pine plank floors and windows that span the length of the dining room and bar, is a family oriented restaurant with entertainment on Friday and Saturday. A limited menu is prepared right on the deck during the summer.

Chef Carlo Valdiserra is serious about food: He grows his own herbs in his home garden and freezes them for year-round use in his restaurant kitchen. David says that Carlo is becoming famous in the area for his lobster bisque and his fish and chips (served with malt vinegar); these are secret recipes that only he knows and won't disclose.

David says the view from *Harbour Seal* "is nice during the day, even better at night. The 4th of July fireworks are shot from a barge right outside on the river, so make a reservation as soon as you know the date. A band performs on the deck. It's a real celebration."

SUNSET CHICKEN

8 oz. boneless chicken breast
¼ C. olive oil
2 garlic cloves, minced
½ C. Chardonnay or other dry white wine
4 or 5 sun dried tomatoes, chopped

2 broccoli spears, chopped
2 leaves of fresh basil, chopped fine
Pinch of fresh chopped parsley
Pinch of salt
Pinch of black pepper

Cooked rice or angel hair pasta

Grill the chicken breast.

After the chicken breast is grilled, dice it into bite-sized pieces; about 2".

Heat the oil in a large pan and quickly sauté the garlic.

Add the chicken, wine, sun dried tomatoes, broccoli, basil, parsley, salt, and pepper.

Sauté for about 3 or 4 minutes, just long enough to get the chicken hot because it is already cooked.

Serve over rice or angel hair pasta.

Serves one

EILEEN'S SCALLOPS AND LOBSTER

1 cooked lobster
6 sea scallops
Flour for dusting
Oil for sautéing
½ stick butter
Pinch of chopped garlic
Pinch of chopped parsley
Pinch of fresh chopped thyme
½ C. sherry wine
Cooked rice or pasta

Remove the lobster meat from the shells and then set it aside.

Lightly flour the scallops.

Heat some oil in a pan and quickly sauté the floured scallops.

Melt the butter in a new pan and add the garlic, parsley, thyme, lobster meat, and the scallops.

Simmer until hot, then add the sherry wine.

Continue to simmer until the sherry has reached the same temperature as the other ingredients.

Serve with rice or pasta.

Serves one

VINAIGRETTE DRESSING

¼ C. balsamic vinegar
¼ C. white wine vinegar
½ C. olive oil
1 t. fresh minced garlic
1 t. fresh chopped
parsley

1 t. fresh chopped
oregano
1 t. fresh chopped basil
1 t. salt
1 t. crushed red pepper

Mix everything together well.

Add more oil and vinegar if it is too spicy for
your taste.

The dressing can be used right away.

Yields one cup

―――――――――――――

*Harbour Seal's recipes were created
by Chef Carlo Valdiserra*

Noank

Noank is a village on a small, vaguely ear-shaped peninsula at the western edge of the Mystic River Harbor. With water on three sides and the double-tracked railroad corridor cutting it off on the northwest, Noank has an isolated feeling, much like an island. Although farm lots were laid out around 1713, there were only 13 houses there in 1825; it was not extensively settled until the middle of the 19th century.

The 1868 Morgan's Point Light-house, at the tip of Noank on Pearl Street, is a 2½ story granite ashlar structure surmounted by a short octagonal tower. It is now a residence and the tower's lantern has been removed. Noank's chief landmark is the Baptist Church, perched on the highest point of land in the village.

Around 1900 Noank began to receive summer residents from New York and other urban areas; publisher George Putnam married Amelia Earhart in the house at 43 Church Street.

FISHERMAN RESTAURANT
937 Groton Long Point Rd., Noank
(860) 536-1717

The big black anchor is the first thing diners see as they pull up to the *Fisherman Restaurant*. Inside, nautical artifacts hug the walls: lobster pots, block and tackle, fishing poles and more — anything having to do with fishing.

Owner Tom Tsagarakis describes the *Fisherman* as casually elegant — suitable for every diner's need. His goal is to serve good food at a decent price in a friendly atmosphere.

He says he tries to strike a balance between people who 'want to eat' and those 'who want to dine'. Children are given crayons and a picture of the *Fisherman's* fish logo to color while they await their meals. Their parents will enjoy gazing out at the views of Palmer's Cover and Fisher's Island Sound.

Fans of Hemingway's <u>Old Man and the Sea</u> will want to take a few moments and linger to appreciate the original pen and ink drawings interpreting the story that adorn one entire wall.

Continuing with the fishing theme, Tom says the *Fisherman's* motto is "It just takes one taste and you'll be hooked."

216

STRAWBERRY AMARETTO SALAD DRESSING

1 C. mayonnaise
1 C. sour cream
6 oz. Amaretto (the good stuff!)
3 oz. Creme de Almond

3 oz. strawberry liqueur or strawberry schnapps
3 T. lemon juice
3 T. olive oil
2 T. poppy seeds

Combine all of the ingredients.

Best if refrigerated overnight.

Yields one quart

Fisherman's recipes were created by Chef James Bennett, Jr.

LOBSTER MADEIRA

1 C. heavy cream
3 oz. mushrooms,
quartered
½ t. minced garlic
¼ C. Madeira wine
2 T. lobster juice
(packing juices)

4 - 5 oz. cooked lobster
meat
1 t. chopped parsley
3 oz. cooked linguini,
kept warm

Combine the first 5 ingredients in a sauce pan.

Bring to a boil.

While it is simmering, scrape the sides and
bottom of the pan with a rubber spatula.

The sauce will thicken.

When it just starts to turn a light shade of grey,
add the lobster meat and continue to simmer until
the lobster is hot.

Pour over the warm pasta and garnish with the
chopped parsley.

Serves two

BREAD PUDDING
WITH BOURBON SAUCE

BREAD PUDDING

4 whole eggs
½ C. sugar
3 C. milk
1 t. cinnamon
½ t. nutmeg
1 cap vanilla extract

1 cap lemon extract
1 pinch of salt
½ C. raisins
1 loaf unsliced white
bread, sliced ¾" thick
(best if one-day-old)

Line the bottom of a baking dish with the raisins.

Lay the bread over the raisins, with the edges overlapping.

Combine the first 8 ingredients and pour over the bread, making sure to soak it well.

Bake at 375° for 45 to 60 minutes.

BOURBON SAUCE

4 oz. butter
½ C. sugar
3 T. Jim Beam bourbon

1 cap vanilla extract
1 egg
Optional: whipped cream

Melt the butter and sugar in a sauce pan until the sugar begins to caramelize and forms a thick sauce.

Add the bourbon and flame. *(Continued...)*

219

Whisk until the alcohol is evaporated. (Flame will go out.)

Cool briefly.

Add the vanilla extract and egg, whisking well.

While the bread pudding is still warm, portion into bowls and spoon bourbon sauce over.

Top with whipped cream, if desired.

Serves four to six

Brown bread, a mixture of two parts cornmeal and one part rye, was the bread eaten by the majority of colonists.

ABBOTT'S LOBSTER IN THE ROUGH
117 Pearl St., Noank
(203) 536-7719

Abbott's Lobster in the Rough has become a summer tradition for thousands of people. Established 50 years ago by Ernie Abbott, Jerry and Ruth Mears bought the business in 1979. Jerry has retired and now Ruth and daughter Deirdre are co-owners of this casual, friendly, boisterous restaurant where alcohol is bring-your-own. Situated right on the ocean's edge, *Abbott's* is only open from May through Columbus Day because, as the Mears say, "the business is totally dependent on the vagaries of New England weather."

Diners can choose between eating indoors or outside at one of the colorful red or green or blue picnic tables that dot the oyster shell spackled grass. While *Abbott's* serves more than lobsters, their lobsters have made them famous. Jerry says their cooking process is "utterly different from other places." They use special cookers originally designed by Ernie — the lobster never sees water. More than 80 tons of lobsters are introduced to the cooker each season. *Abbott's* now has a little "sister" restaurant: just a bit down the road you'll find *Costello's* nestled among the docks; it has a new upper deck and expansive ocean views (also seasonal).

ABBOTT'S NOANK STYLE CLAM CHOWDER

4 oz. salt pork
1 t. sliced garlic
1 T. finely minced onion
1 T. flour
2 C. clam broth
1 C. water
1 bay leaf
¼ C. celery, finely chopped
¼ C. carrots, finely chopped

¼ C. fresh parsley chopped
½ lb. chopped steamed clams
¼ t. dried rosemary
½ t. dried leaf thyme
1 t. salt
¼ t. white pepper
¼ t. sherry wine
1 T. butter
1½ C. diced potatoes

Cut salt pork into cubes.

Place them in a small sauce pan and over medium heat, cook until all fat is rendered.

Remove and discard pieces of pork.

In same sauce pan, sauté garlic in rendered fat until browned. Remove and discard garlic.

Add onions and sauté until translucent.

Gradually sprinkle in flour, stirring.

Cook 1 minute, continuing to stir.

Remove from heat and set aside. *(Continued...)*

Place clam broth and water in a large kettle over medium heat.

When liquid begins to simmer, whisk in onion-flour mixture.

Add remaining ingredients.

Reduce heat to low and simmer gently for 30 minutes.

Remove bay leaf.

Cover and refrigerate 24 hours to allow flavors to meld.

Heat and serve.

Yields 1 quart, four to six servings

Recipe created by the late Ernie Abbott, founder of Abbott's, and his wife Doris, at least 50 years ago.

MUSTARD DILL SAUCE

⅓ C. minced dill   ½ C. sugar
1 C. Dijon mustard   ⅓ C. white vinegar
1 T. dry mustard   1 C. vegetable oil

Remove the leaves from the stems of dill and put them in a food processor.

Chop the dill in the processor.

Remove the chopped dill to a dish and reserve.

Put the mustards, sugar, and vinegar in the processor. Mix.

Slowly, drop by drop, beat in the oil.

The dressing will become thick.

Stir in the reserved dill.

Store in the refrigerator.

---

*Recipe created by Ruth Mears,
co-owner of Costello's and Abbott's;
recipe is used exclusively as a dipping
sauce at Costello's*

Mystic

Mystic is on Long Island Sound across from the eastern end of Long Island. It is divided by the Mystic River, which is actually an arm of the Sound; the section on the west bank is in Groton and east bank portion is in Stonington. The bridge over the river is on U.S. Route 1 (Main Street) and it runs through the districts.

The first bridge in 1819 was wooden and was drawn by oxen eastward to open it for ships. The present bridge, built in 1924, has an 85 feet span and is lifted by two 200-ton concrete counterweights cased in metal shields.

The community of Mystic developed because of 19th century ship building and associated activity along the Mystic River. Most of the actual shipbuilding was on the east bank. The west bank was given over to a commercial strip, some ship building, and other industrial activity, and primarily, to many fine homes.

S&P OYSTER CO.
1 Holmes St., Mystic
(860) 536-2674

S&P Oyster Co. is located just before (or after) one of the last drawbridges in Connecticut — the bridge spanning the Mystic River as it makes its journey to the Sound.

This establishment has two personalities: the downstairs dining room is non-smoking and more family oriented according to the general manager, Cathleen Marriott. Upstairs, the bar hugs the length of one wall and smoking is acceptable. Both dining rooms' windows look out upon the harbor with its yachts and sailing crafts and views of Mystic Seaport in the distance.

If you're upstairs, remember to look up at the blue and white sails that cover the ceiling: the sails are from the nearby Coast Guard Academy. At night, when the light shines through them, the effect is quite unusual.

Cathleen describes *S&P Oyster Co.* as friendly, fun, and casual. But this restaurant, where simple New England seafood is the specialty, is versatile — it is also the choice for wedding rehearsal dinners and business meetings.

Consider stopping in when the drawbridge opens — which is every quarter on the hour — that is, if you even need a reason.

DICKY'S FAMOUS CHILI

1 lb. hamburg
3 T. olive oil
1½ Spanish onions, chopped
½ C. chopped garlic
1 t. cumin

4 T. chili powder
3 C. canned diced tomatoes
4 C. canned kidney beans, drained
2 T. beef base

Cook the onions and garlic in the olive oil for about 5 minutes, until the onions are translucent.

Add the cumin and chili powder.

Add the hamburg, stirring constantly, until well done.

Add the tomatoes, beans, and beef base.

Cook for 1 hour.

Yields one gallon

The "Connecticut Courant" was started by Thomas Green in 1764. It is the oldest continuously produced American newspaper.

BISQUE

½ lb. butter
5½ oz. lobster stock (boil
off shells)
2½ T. paprika

1 C. flour
4 qts. half and half
2½ T. sherry wine

Melt the butter down.

Add the lobster stock and the paprika.

Add the flour to make a roux.

Add all of the half and half and using a large
wire whisk, stir vigorously to dissolve the roux.

Add the sherry wine.

Let simmer about 45 minutes.

Cool completely before refrigerating.

Yields one gallon

---

*Jonathan Trumbull became governor of
Connecticut in 1769 — before the Revolution
— and held office for 15 years during the
formation of the new nation.*

BOUILLABAISSE

2½ lbs. fish scraps (tuna, scrod, salmon, swordfish)
1 t. olive oil
¾ lb. butter
½ stalk celery, chopped
1 Spanish onion, chopped
4 T. garlic, chopped
1½ C. clam juice or fish stock
2 T. Worcestershire sauce
1 T. Tabasco pepper sauce

¼ bulb fennel, chopped
2½ t. chopped fresh basil
2½ t. oregano
2½ t. tarragon
½ bay leaf
3½ C. canned diced tomatoes
1¾ C. tomato puree
2 T. lemon juice
¼ t. pepper or to taste
Water

Sauté the celery, onions, and garlic in the olive oil and butter in a soup kettle.

Add the fish stock, Worcestershire sauce, Tabasco pepper sauce, fennel, basil, oregano, tarragon, and bay leaf.

Simmer for about 10 minutes.

Add the fish scraps, tomatoes and tomato puree, lemon juice, pepper, and enough water to make your kettle ¾ full.

Let cook for about 45 minutes; remove bay leaf.

Yields one gallon

229

XXX

FLOOD TIDE at the Mystic Inn
Junction Routes 1 and 27, Mystic
(860) 536-8140

The *Flood Tide* at the Mystic Inn, where the menu is primarily 'French Continental with an American accent', is renowned for its unique table-side preparations of favorites like Caesar Salad, Chateaubriand, Bananas Foster and even flaming coffees.

Flood Tide emphasizes the total dining experience: from the water views of Mystic Harbor and Long Island Sound visible from both the upper and lower dining rooms to the visual presentation of the food, this restaurant, located on thirteen acres of wooded hillside and owned by innkeepers and sisters Jody Dyer and Nancy Gray since 1963, is ideal for people who want to dine for two or three hours. But that doesn't mean diners must stay that long! Breakfast and lunch buffets are offered daily in season (April — December) as well as an afternoon tea. *Flood Tide* also hosts specialty dinners on the major holidays.

Bob Tripp, the Executive Chef, and a father himself, notes that *Flood Tide* is "a nice place for children who are looking for a formal dining experience" — along with views of Fisher's Island at the mouth of Long Island Sound — to become familiar with more sophisticated dining.

230

CREPE FILLED
WITH LOBSTER MADEIRA

6 medium mushrooms, sliced thin	12 oz. freshly picked lobster meat, 1" dice
1 t. finely minced shallots	3 oz. Madeira wine
1 t. finely chopped fresh parsley	10 oz. heavy cream
	6 crepe shells
2 T. butter	Fresh dill for garnish

Sauté the mushrooms, shallots, and parsley in the whole butter on medium heat in a large sauté pan until golden brown.

Add the lobster and the Madeira wine.

Reduce until almost dry.

Add the heavy cream and reduce until the sauce coats the back of a spoon.

Fill the crepe shells with the filling, roll, and top with the sauce.

Garnish with the dill sprigs.

Serves six

SHRIMP PROVENÇALE

2 T. extra virgin olive oil
10 colossal shrimp,
peeled and deveined,
leaving tail on
Flour for dusting
1 t. fresh chopped garlic
1 t. fresh chopped parsley
1 t. fresh chopped basil

½ C. diced, skinned
tomatoes with juice
3 large artichoke hearts,
cut in quarters
Juice from half a lemon
¼ C. dry white wine
2 oz. softened butter
Angel hair pasta or
white rice, cooked

Add the oil to a large sauté pan; heat the pan on medium high heat.

Dust shrimp in flour and place in the pre-heated pan.

Sauté until golden brown on 1 side, about 3 minutes; turn over, then add the garlic, parsley, and basil.

Sauté for 1 minute, then add tomatoes and artichoke hearts and sauté for another minute.

Add lemon juice and white wine; reduce until almost dry. Turn heat down if needed.

Remove from heat and stir in softened butter to make the sauce. Serve over pasta or rice.

Serves two

CHOCOLATE FONDUE
WITH FRESH FRUIT

8 oz. imported semi-
sweet chocolate, cut in
½" pieces
¼ C. heavy cream

2 T. Grand Marnier
2 T. kirschwasser
¼ t. cinnamon
¼ t. nutmeg

Bite-sized fruit pieces and berries

On medium heat, melt the chocolate and cream
in a medium sauté pan until smooth.

Add both liqueurs and spices.

Reduce until thick, about 3 minutes.

Serve with bite-sized fruit pieces and berries.

Serves four

---

*Gurdon Saltonstall, Connecticut's 10th
governor, was the first American-born
governor. He was born in Haverhill,
Massachusetts in 1666.*

Stonington

This coastline of Pequot Indian country was first mapped by Adriaen Block from Holland in 1614. The first settlers in 1649 were William and Anna Chesebrough at Wequetequock Cove. The next year Thomas Stanton built a trading post on the Pawcatuck River. Two years later came Walter Palmer, Thomas Miner, and Captain George Denison. John Gallup and Robert Park settled in the Mystic area soon afterwards.

In 1658 Massachusetts claimed the town, naming it Southerton. Governor John Winthrop, Jr. obtained the Connecticut Charter from England in 1662, which set the boundaries of the town. It was renamed Mystic in 1665 and Stonington in 1666.

Men of Stonington repulsed a British naval attack on the town, both in 1775 and 1814. The old trades of shipbuilding, whaling, sealing, and the railroad-steamboat terminal have been replaced by light manufacturing and commercial fishing. Today, Stonington's past maritime glory is reflected in the relics of her Mystic Seaport and Old Lighthouse Museum.

BOOM
194 Water St. at Dodson Boatyard, Stonington
(860) 535-2588

Jean Fuller comes from a "big sailing family" which explains her choice for a restaurant name: *Boom*. The boom is the long spar used to extend the foot of a sail.

Jean describes *Boom*, with its new mahogany bar, as a restaurant that mixes the traditional with the innovative; it's sophisticated but with good value; and it attracts both dock mechanics and women wearing Gucci jewelry. While it's not a suit and tie restaurant, they do strive for a sophisticated edge.

Stonington is home to the last commercial fishing fleet in Connecticut. Jean and her sister Franny developed *Boom's* menu with an eye focused on the fresh catch brought in by the *Patty Jo* down the street. The Stonington area is blessed with farmers markets, an advantage not overlooked by the sisters.

Boom has one coming service that is especially imaginative and will be appreciated by boaters: *Boom Raw Bar Girls* will ride around the harbor in a whaler delivering food to boats — and those who called ahead to Dodson Boatyard won't even have to step ashore to enjoy *Boom's* cuisine.

LIGHTLY BATTERED FRIED OYSTERS WITH LEMON-TARRAGON MIGNONETTE

36 shucked oysters   Mignonette

MIGNONETTE

1 T. minced shallot   3 T. lemon juice
1 t. minced garlic   ¼ C. extra-virgin olive oil
½ C. packed fresh   Pinch salt
tarragon, chopped fine   5 turns of black pepper
½ C. red wine vinegar

Place the shallots and garlic in a mixing bowl.

Add the red wine vinegar and lemon juice.

Let stand for 5 minutes.

Add remaining ingredients, *except the oil.*

Slowly whisk in the olive oil.

Let sit for at least 1 hour to develop the flavors.

ASSEMBLY

EGG WASH

4 eggs   ½ C. milk   Salt and pepper

Beat eggs with milk seasoned with salt and pepper.

(Continued...)

SEASONED FLOUR

1 C. flour	**1 t. cayenne pepper**
2 T. paprika	**Salt and pepper**

Mix the Seasoned Flour ingredients together.

Heat the frying oil to 350°.

Dip the oysters in the egg wash.

Next, dip them in the Seasoned Flour.

Fry them until they are golden brown.

Serve with the Mignonette.

Serves six

---

*Boom's recipes were created
by the restaurant's staff*

ROASTED BUTTERNUT SQUASH SOUP WITH SAMBUCA

2 medium butternut squash, peeled and cubed large	1 sweet potato, peeled and cubed
1 white onion, quartered	¼ C. Sambuca liqueur
1 carrot, peeled and sliced	Salt and pepper to taste
	Olive oil

Preheat oven to 450°.

Lightly coat vegetables with olive oil and roast the vegetables until they are tender.

Put the vegetables in a soup pot and cover with cold water.

Bring to a boil and reduce to a simmer for 15 minutes.

Remove from the heat and puree until smooth in a blender.

Add salt and pepper to taste.

Finish with Sambuca liqueur.

For a tasty garnish, reserve butternut squash seeds, clean, toss with a little olive oil, salt and pepper, and roast in the oven until brown and crispy. Sprinkle on top of soup and serve.

BOSC PEAR SALAD WITH TOASTED WALNUTS, DANISH BLUE CHEESE, AND LEMON VINAIGRETTE

2 bosc pears	Mesclun greens
½ C. toasted walnuts	Lemon Vinaigrette
¾ C. Danish or other high quality blue cheese	

LEMON VINAIGRETTE

¼ C. fresh squeezed lemon juice	¾ C. extra-virgin olive oil
1 T. rice wine vinegar	3 turns of black pepper
Pinch of salt	

Mix everything together.

ASSEMBLY

Preparing the walnuts
Lightly coat the walnuts with olive oil and season with salt and pepper. Bake in a 350° oven for 5 minutes.

Slice the pears and toss them along with the blue cheese and walnuts and mesclun greens.

Lightly dress the salad with the Lemon Vinaigrette and serve.

SKIPPER'S DOCK
66 Water St., Stonington
(860) 535-8544

Skipper's Dock is a traveler's first (or last) chance to dine on the water along Connecticut's coast. Dining 'on the water' is not an exaggeration because the deck literally extends over Long Island Sound.

Skipper's Dock is at the very end of an easy to miss driveway — and its view of the ocean and Fisher's Island is spectacular.

This restaurant's interior is divided into two sections: the bar-smoking side where entertainment is frequently provided on Friday and Sunday; and the non-smoking casual dining room. But the biggest lure is the 100 seat deck.

There is a camaraderie among the staff at *Skipper's Dock* that enhances the dining experience. Be sure to greet manager Kimberly Ward whose husband, Norm, is the executive chef; Norm makes culinary magic with his sous chef, Bart Chamberlain. They say the menu ranges from 'California cuisine to New England boiled dinners'. Susi Ward (no relation to Kimberly and Norm) ensures the bar runs smoothly. But most importantly, keep an eye open for John Hewes because he's the owner of this appetizing place. (Open mid-May to the end of September)

240

BLACKENED FISH

1½" thick swordfish or	1 T. black pepper
tuna steaks	2 T. dry basil
1 C. paprika	2 T. dry oregano
1 T. white pepper	2 T. dry thyme
1 T. kosher salt	1 or 2 T. garlic salt
1 T. cayenne pepper	3 T. oil

Mix the spices and herbs together.

Add the oil to a cast iron pan.

While the pan is heating up, dip the fish into the paprika mixture, being careful to coat both sides well.

When the pan is very hot, transfer the fish to the pan.

Sear the fish for 1 minute on each side.

Transfer the pan with the fish to a 350° oven for 10 minutes or until the fish is firm to the touch.

Serves two

BOUILLABAISSE

1 leek stalk, bottom part, chopped
4 C. whole peeled tomatoes, chopped
Pinch of saffron
2 T. oil
1 t. parsley
2 T. clam base or seafood base

1 t. fennel seeds
1 C. white wine
3 C. water
1 t. chopped garlic
2 clams
2 large shrimp
1 lobster tail, cut in half
2 lobster claws

Sauté the leeks in the oil.

Add everything *except the seafood.*

Let it simmer for 30 minutes.

Add the clams, shrimp, and lobster.

Continue to simmer until the clams have opened and the shellfish is cooked.

Serves two

Sherwood Island in Westport was the first state park in Connecticut.

SHRIMP AND BROCCOLI PASTA

1 lb. rotini pasta
12 medium shrimp,
peeled and deveined
¼ C. olive oil
2 C. cooked broccoli
flowerets
2 T. chopped fresh basil

¼ C. red roasted
peppers, sliced
¼ C. sliced sun dried
tomatoes
2 T. chopped garlic
Salt and pepper to taste

Cook the pasta according to package directions.

When the pasta is just about ready, sauté the shrimp
in the oil for 1 minute on each side.

Add the broccoli, basil, roasted peppers, sun dried
tomatoes, and garlic.

Mix in the cooked pasta.

Salt and pepper to taste, and serve.

Serves two

---

*Captain John Smith gave New England its
name. The whole north continent had been
called Nova Albion and Nova Britannia; the
New England region was called Norumbega.*

243

Alphabetical Listing of Restaurants
with Directions from I-95

Abbott's Lobster in the Rough
117 Pearl St., Noank *North:* Exit 89 (Allyn St.) to Rt. 215*; *South:* Exit 90, to Rt. 215* Follow 215 to Noank; *L* on Mosher to T-junction; *L* on Main St.; 1st *R* onto Pearl

Allen's Clam & Lobster House
191 Hillspoint Rd., Westport *North:* Exit 18; *L* off exit ramp;* *South: R* off exit ramp; **L* at 2nd light, Greens Farms; *L* at stop sign (Hillspoint)

Amarante's
62 Cove St., New Haven *North:* Exit 50, *R* at 2nd light, Townsend; *R* at 2nd light, Lighthouse;* *South:* Exit 51; *L* at 3rd light, Townsend; *R* at 3rd light, Lighthouse; * 5th *R* into parking lot

Aqua
34 Riverside Dr., Clinton: Exit 63 to Rt. 81S to Rt. 1 to Grove St. to Riverside Dr.

Atlantis Restaurant
500 Steamboat Rd., Greenwich: Exit 3, follow signs to Bruce Museum

Beach Street Waterfront Grille
343 Beach St., West Haven *North:* Exit 44; *L* at bottom of exit; *L* at 2nd light, First Ave.;* *South:* Exit 43; *L* at end of exit;* *follow to water

Beachhead
3 Cosey Beach Av., East Haven *North:* Exit 51, Frontage Rd.; *R* at 2nd light: Hemingway Ave./Rt. 142* *South:* Exit 51, Frontage Rd.; *L* at 2nd light; *continue 2½ miles to Cosey Beach Av.; *L*, go to end

Bill's Seafood
Boston Post Rd., Westbrook *Exit 65*; to Rt. 1/Boston Post Rd. (at "Singing Bridge")

Black Duck Cafe
605 Riverside Av., Westport *North:* Exit 17; *R* on Saugatuck Av.; *L* at light on Park;* *South:* Exit 17; straight off exit onto Park;* quick jog *R* and *L* into driveway (look for Coastwise Marina) to restaurant

Bloodroot
85 Ferris St., Bridgeport *Exit 24;* south on

Black Rock Tpk.; *L* on Fairfield Av.; *R* on Ellsworth Av.; 2nd *L* on Thurton St.; 1st *R* on Harbor Av., 3rd *R* on Ferris St.

Boom
194 Water St. at Dodson Boatyard, Stonington *Exit 91,* follow signs to Stonington Borough; cross viaduct bridge; look straight ahead for Dodson Boatyard

Captain's Cove
1 Bostwick Av., Bridgeport *Exit 26,* Wordin; follow signs

Captain's Galley
19 Beach St., West Haven *North:* Exit 44; *L* at bottom of exit; *L* at 2nd light, First Av.* *South:* Exit 43; *L* at end of exit;* follow to water

Chart House
100 South Water St., New Haven *North:* Exit 44, bear *R* off ramp; *R* at light; *R* at stop sign (Howard);* *South:* Exit 45, bear *L*; *L* at end; *R* at stop sign (Howard)* *go to end

244

Constantine's
252 Main St., Niantic
North: Exit 74; *R* at
end of exit; *R* on Rt.
161;* *South:* Exit 74,
R. at end of exit; *R* on
Rt. 161.*Follow 161
until it intersects with
156; *R* on 156 which is
Main St. in Niantic

Costa Azzura
72 Broadway, Milford
Exit 34 (Rt. 1), Milford;
keep in right lane of
exit ramp to end; *R* on
Rt. 1; *L* at 3rd light
(Naugatuck Av.); turn *R*
1 block after 4th light,
onto Broadway

Crab Shell
46 Southfield Av.,
Stamford *North:* Exit 7;
Greenwich Av.; *R* at
end of exit onto Green-
wich Av.; straight thru
light at intersection of
Greenwich/Selleck/
Southfield *South:* Exit
7, Atlantic St.; straight
on access road at end of
exit ramp until intersec-
tion with Washington
Blvd; *L* on Washington;
R at 3rd light, Palaski;
straight onto Greenwich
Ave; straight on South-
field

Dock & Dine
Saybrook Point, Old
Saybrook *North:* Exit
67; bear *R* onto Rt. 154;
L at 3rd light; continue
on 154.* *South:* Exit

68; bear *R* on Rt. 1 at
bottom of ramp; *L* at
1st light, Rt. 154. *L* at
2nd light *Follow to
water.

Dolphin's Cove
421 Seaview Av.,
Bridgeport *Exit 29*,
Stratford Av. Seaview
Av. toward water

Fisherman
937 Groton Long Point,
Noank *North:* Exit 88,
R at bottom of exit on
Rt. 117; *L* on Rt. 1;
bear *R* on Rt. 215;
follow 2 miles* *South:*
Exit 89, *L* onto Allyn;
go 2 miles, thru Rt. 1
light; *R* on Noank Rd.,
2½ miles to end; *L* on
Rt. 215* to restaurant

Flood Tide
Junction Rts. 1 and 27,
Mystic *Exit 90*; south
on Rt. 27 for 2 miles; *L*
onto Rt. 1 North.

Harbour Seal
359 Thames St., Groton
North: Exit 85, Thames
St. *R* at end of ramp*
South: Exit 87, left exit
(Clarence Sharp Hwy.);
take 1st exit, follow
Downtown Groton/
Bridge St. signs; *L* at
stop sign (Bridge St.);
straight thru traffic
lights; Bridge St. turns
into Thames St.

Hurricane's
80 Seaview Av.,

Norwalk *North:* Exit
14; go *R*; straight to
intersection of Water
and Washington Sts.,
cross bridge* *South:*
Exit 16; *R* on East Av.,
continue until it's one-
way; con-tinue; *L* at
stop sign onto Seaview
*restaurant on right

Jimmie's of Savin Rock
5 Rock St., West Haven
North: Exit 42; *L* at end
of ramp;* *South:* Exit
42; *R* at end of ramp;*
go to end

Knapp's Landing
520 Sniffen Ln., Strat-
ford *North:* Exit 30,
straight onto Lordship
Blvd.; bear *L* on Access
Rd. at fork at 7th light;
follow to end; facing
Allied Signal, turn *R* on
Main St.; follow factory
building and take 1st *L*
on Sniffens Ln.* *South:*
Exit 31 (South Av.); *L*
at end of ramp, go un-
der thruway, on South
Av., past stop sign to *R*
at light, Main St.; *L* at
at 8th light, Sniffens
Ln. *continue to end

Lighthouse Inn
6 Guthrie Pl., New
London *North:* Exit 82;
R on Broad; *R* at 2nd
light, Coleman St.*
South: Exit 83; *L* on
Coleman *Follow Cole-
man to end; *L* on Bank;
R. on Montauck at 2nd

245

light; follow to end; *R* on Pequot; 2nd *R* on Guthrie Place

Mangia Mangia
215 Main St., Niantic *Exit 74*, R on Rt. 161; go about 3 miles; last building on right at intersection of Rts. 156 and 161.

Marnicks
10 Washington Pkwy., Stratford *Exit 30*; follow signs to airport; *R* at 2nd stop sign (Washington); go to end

Outriggers
at Foot of Broad St., Stratford *North:* Exit 32 (W. Broad St.), straight off exit; *L* at 2nd light, Main St.; quick *R* at light, Broad St.* *South:* Exit 32; *L* off ramp; *L* at light; *follow straight to Brewer's Marina

Oyster River Tavern
38 Ocean Av., West Haven *North:* Exit 41; turn *R;* * *South:* Exit 41, turn *L;** go to end; turn *R.*; restaurant on corner on right
Paradise Bar & Grill
78 Southfield Av., Stamford *North:* Exit 7; *R* on Greenwich Av. at end of ramp; straight thru light at intersection of Greenwich/Selleck/ Southfield streets *South:* Exit 7; straight

on access road at end of ramp; continue to Washington Blvd.; turn *L*; at 3rd light, *R* on Pulaski; straight past stop sign onto Greenwich Ave, thru light onto Southfield Ave.

Pasta Paul's
223 Thames St., Groton *North:* Exit 85 (Thames St.), stay *R* at end of ramp on Thames *South:* Exit 87, left exit (Clarence Sharp Hwy.); take 1st exit, follow Downtown Groton/Bridge St. signs; *L* at stop sign; go thru all lights; Bridge St. becomes Thames St.

Rusty Scupper
501 Long Wharf Dr., New Haven *North:* Exit 46 (Long Wharf); *L* off exit, straight for ½ mile* *South:* Exit 46; *R* at end of exit; *R* at next light (under thruway); *L* at next light; go about ¼ mile *restaurant on *R*

S&P Oyster Co.
1 Holmes St., Mystic *North:* Exit 89 (Allyn St.); *R* off exit, follow Allyn thru blinking stop light; *L* at light, Main St.; thru downtown Mystic, over the drawbridge; *L* at flagpole onto Holmes St.; quick *L* into parking lot *South:* Exit 90; *L* at end of ramp onto Rt. 27S; at

3rd light (Mystic Seaport), Holmes is 3rd street down on right; *R* on Holmes.

Sabbia Ristorante Mediterraneo
233 Hillspoint Rd., Westport *North:* Exit 18; *L* off exit ramp* *South:* Exit 18; *R* off exit ramp* *L* at 2nd light (Greens Farm Rd.); *L* at 4-way stop sign (Hillspoint Rd.)

Sam's Dockside
Block Island Rd., Branford I-95 to Branford Rt. 146 exit; follow 146 to Bruce & Johnson Marina. Turn in.

Seascape
14 Beach Dr., Stratford *Exit 30*; follow signs to airport, pass airport; *R* at 2nd stop sign (Washington); *L* at end of road; 2nd building over

Skipper's Dock
66 Water St., Stonington *Exit 91;* follow signs to Stonington Borough; cross viaduct bridge to Stonington Center; watch for Skipper's Dock sign and entrance *(Easy to miss!)*

Sono Seafood
100 Water St., Norwalk *North:* Exit 14; go *R;* go to intersection of Water and Washington Sts.;

immediate *R* before bridge. *South:* Exit 16; go *L* for ½ mile; continue until intersection; *R* over Washington St. Bridge; immediate *L* on Water St.

Splash Pacific Rim Grill
260 Compo Rd. South, Westport *North:* Exit 17; straight off ramp; *L* at stop sign, Riverside Av.; 1st *R* over bridge, Bridge St.; *R* at light onto Compo Rd. S. (Rt. 136)* *South:* Exit 18, Sherwood Island Connector Rd.; bear *R* on ramp; *L* at 2nd light, Greens Farms Rd.; go thru 2 stop signs; *L* at light, Compo Rd. S. (Rt. 136); pass under thruway and RR bridges. *Enter Longshore Club Park; follow signs for Inn at Longshore/Splash; straight at fork, continue to end; *L* at stop sign to parking lot

Steamer's Bar & Grill
Whitfield St., Guilford *North:* Exit 58, turn *R** *South:* Exit 58, turn *L**
*Continue until facing town green; turn *R*, quick *L* on Whitfield

Stone House
506 Whitfield St., Guilford *North:* Exit 58, turn *R** *South:* Exit 58, turn *L** Follow until facing town green; make a *R* and a quick *L* on Whitfield St.

Sunset Rib Co.
378 Rope Ferry Rd., Waterford *Exit 74; R* at end of ramp onto Rt. 161; continue to end; *L* on Rt. 156; go across bridge; *L* at stop sign

Terra Mar Grille at Old Saybrook Point Inn and Spa, 2 Bridge St., Old Saybrook *North:* Exit 67; bear *R* on Rt. 154; *L* at 3rd light; continue on 154* *South:* Exit 68; bear *R* on Rt. 1 at bottom of ramp; *L* at 1st light onto Rt. 154; *L* at 2nd light; continue on 154; * to water

The Restaurant at Rowayton Seafood
89 Rowayton Av., Rowayton *North:* Exit 12, *R* at end of ramp on Rt. 136;* *South:* Exit 11, bear *R* off ramp onto Rt. 1; *R* at 3rd light (Rt. 136);* 1½ miles to stop sign; continue 500 yds.

Unk's on the Bay
361 Rope Ferry Rd., Waterford North: Exit 74; *R* at end of ramp onto Rt. 161; continue to end; turn *L* on Rt. 156; cross bridge; *L* at stop sign

Upper Deck
130 Pequot Av., New London *North:* Exit 82, Broad St.; *R* on Broad St.; *R* at 2nd light, Coleman St.* *South:* Exit 83; turn *L* on Coleman * follow to end; *L* on Bank St.; go thru 5 lights, *R* on Howard (at Columbus Square); go to end, bear *L* under train trestle, onto Pequot; go ¼ mile

Water's Edge
1525 Boston Post Rd. Westbrook *North:* Exit 65; *R* on Rt. 153;* *South:* Exit 65; *L* on Rt. 153 *L* at 2nd light onto Rt. 1

The Wharf
West Wharf Rd., Madison *North:* Exit 61, *R* off exit onto Rt. 79;* *South:* Exit 61, *L* off exit onto Rt. 79; *R* at 3rd light (Boston Post Rd./Rt. 1); 3rd *L* on West Wharf Rd. (golf course is on right as you turn); follow to the end

Note: While I tried to be accurate, it's a good idea to call the restaurant to verify the directions, especially if you're unfamiliar with the area — and to confirm the place is still open. JS

Guide to Popular Restaurant Services

	Child's Menu	Deck/Patio	Boat Docking Available*	Private Parties	Food-to-Go
Abbott's Lobster in the Rough	X	X	X	X	X
Allen's Clam & Lobster House					
Amarante's	X	X	nearby	X	X
Aqua Restaurant	X	X	X	X	X
Atlantis	X	X	X	X	X
Beach Street Waterfront Grille	X	X		X	X
Beachhead	X	X		X	X
Bill's Seafood	X	X	X		X
Black Duck Cafe	X				X
Bloodroot		X		X	X
Boom		X	X	X	X
Captain's Cove Seaport	X	X	X	X	X
Captain's Galley	X	X		X	X
Chart House	X	X	X	X	X
Constantine's	X			X	X
Costa Azzura	X			X	X
Crab Shell	X	X	X	X	X
Dock & Dine	X	X	X	X	X
Dolphin's Cove	X	X	X	X	X
Fisherman Restaurant	X			X	X
Flood Tide at the Mystic Inn	X	X		X	
Harbour Seal	X	X	X	X	X
Hurricane's	X	X	X	X	X
Jimmie's of Savin Rock	X			X	X
Knapp's Landing	X	X	X	X	X

Guide to Popular Restaurant Services

	Child's Menu	Deck/Patio	Boat Docking Available*	Private Parties	Food-to-Go
Lighthouse Inn	X	X		X	X
Mangia Mangia	X	X		X	X
Marnicks	X				X
Outriggers	X	X	X	X	X
Oyster River Tavern	X	X			X
Paradise Bar & Grill		X	X	X	X
Pasta Paul's Shop	X	X			X
Restaurant at Rowayton Seafood	X	X	X	X	X
Rusty Scupper	X	X		X	X
S & P Oyster Co.	X		X	X	X
Sabbia Ristorante Mediterraneo			X		
Sam's Dockside		X	X		X
Seascape	X			X	X
Skipper's Dock	X	X	X	X	
Sono Seaport Seafood	X	X	X	X	X
Splash Pacific Rim Grill		X	nearby	X	
Steamers Bar & Grill	X		X	X	X
Stone House	X		X	X	X
Sunset Rib Co.	X	X	X	X	
Terra Mar Grille	X		X	X	
Unk's on the Bay	X	X		X	X
Upper Deck	X		X	X	X
Water's Edge	X	X		X	
(The) Wharf	X	X		X	X

* It's best to call the marina for details and availability, not the restaurant

X = yes

Index

251

Notes